Pinch Me

Pinch Me

Waking Up in a 300-Year-Old Italian Farmhouse

Barbara Boyle

SHE WRITES PRESS

Published 2025
Printed in the United States of America
Print ISBN: 978-1-64742-832-7
E-ISBN: 978-1-64742-833-4
Library of Congress Control Number: 2024918846

For information, address:
She Writes Press
1569 Solano Ave #546
Berkeley, CA 94707

Interior Design by Tabitha Lahr
Map Design by Erin Greb

She Writes Press is a division of SparkPoint Studio, LLC.

Names and identifying characteristics have been changed to protect the privacy of certain individuals.

For Nicoletta Gallo and her eternal friendship.
DECEMBER 16, 1978–AUGUST 13, 2022

You may have the universe if I may have Italy.

—GIUSEPPE VERDI, COMPOSER

INTRODUCTION

T rue story. I live in a town that is made of the stuff of fairy tales. There are castles perched atop the hills, stone farmhouses with neat little gardens, carefully planted vineyards and orchards rolling through the valleys, all surrounded in the distance by snowy Alps. But this is not a town of fantasy. Quite the contrary. Honest, sensible, and industrious people live here. They are extraordinarily handsome and generous, but they are humble, hardworking, and just as real as you or I.

The town is Monforte, nestled among the ridges and valleys of Piemonte in Northern Italy, a couple of hours' drive from the cities of Milan and Turin. Piemonte has begun to be discovered by Europeans as a food and wine destination in the last decade or two, but Americans are much less familiar with it, traveling instead to Tuscany and maybe Umbria, when seeking a holiday outside of Italy's beautiful but bustling big cities. Monforte is still very much a small town, and the surrounding countryside feels absolutely pastoral and tranquil. I live with my husband a few miles from Monforte's main piazza in the little commune of Roddino, in a centuries-old farmhouse that we are restoring. Taking this wonderful stone structure apart, virtually stone by stone, and putting it back together to transform it into a home for us, our family, and friends, has been our job, and our passion, for the last few years. And every step of the way, this community has sustained us. We began this adventure not knowing a word of Italian or having any idea of the various laws and protocols that we would encounter, yet the people of Monforte and Piemonte have supported and helped us, each in their own way.

> *Tucked up into the northwest corner of Italy, in the knee of the "boot," Piemonte borders both France and Switzerland and is surrounded on three sides by the Alps; hence the name, Piemonte, or "foot of the mountains."*

Monforte and neighboring Roddino are in an area of Piemonte called the Langhe. Its name means "tongues" and refers to the miles and miles of ridgelines that crisscross the landscape. The roads that run along the ridgelines make for sweepingly scenic driving, in every season. Piemonte stretches south to just a few miles north of the Ligurian Sea, which means the location does not only promise a lovely climate; it also means that on any given day we can visit the snowy mountains or the azure sea and sandy beaches, in just over an hour. Like Camelot, this land is abundant, welcoming, romantic, and beautiful beyond words.

Please come with me on my journey from a busy, modern American life, to an enchanted one in Italy, where every moment, every bite, and every relationship is meant to be enjoyed and dreams really do come true.

CHAPTER ONE

It was Wednesday. Gemma Boeri, proprietor of Osteria Da Gemma, and a select cadre of neighbors were making the hundreds, maybe thousands, of ravioli needed for the restaurant that week, as they always do. At eight thirty on a frosty February morning, there was already a buzz of activity in the room set aside for pasta making. I stood in the doorway, hesitating, unsure of where to go.

Gemma was rolling out the eggy yellow pasta dough into sheets longer than her arm, feeding them back into the roller over and over until she was satisfied that the thickness was perfect for her *ravioli del plin*. A dozen women and two men were gathered around various tables, all deeply immersed in the business of *plin* making, taking the sheets from her and transforming them into perfect little morsels. The Michelin-recognized Osteria Da Gemma is the town of Roddino's greatest treasure, and the pasta is one excellent reason why.

Gemma looked up, caught my eye, and smiled. She welcomed me, an interested observer, into her restaurant, wiping her hands on her apron and offering me a chair to sit and watch, although I was the youngest person in the room and the only one not standing. All the others were hard at work bent over the tables. In turn, each one smiled at me, but their chatter was in the Piemontese dialect, not the Dante's Italian that I had been studying, so I was hopelessly lost trying to follow their conversations. From time to time, someone addressed me directly in traditional Italian, which I appreciated greatly. Gemma offered me a piece of apple torte, still warm from the oven. She always seems happiest when she is offering someone something delicious to eat.

Gemma went back to rolling out the dough, while the women took the sheets of pasta and placed them on lightly floured wooden tables. Using a large spoon and small knife, they expertly scooped out tiny mounds of filling and placed them on the dough in rows, folding the pasta over like a blanket to seal them. Then they cut them into long, thin strips that looked like bumpy snakes and set them aside. Finally, the two men cut the strips apart into individual ravioli. I thought it was unfair that only the men got to do all the cutting. The women told me it was the only task they allowed the men to do.

Plin actually means "pinch" in the Piemontese dialect, and it is in fact that characteristic little pinch that separates these raviolis from all others on Earth. It is also what makes them so incredibly delicious, because in addition to holding in the filling nice and snug, the pinch forms little pockets all around the outside that cradle the ragu or melted butter with sage and Parmesan. The filling is a satisfying combination of cooked greens and vegetables, some roasted veal, maybe rabbit and pork, and a bit of Parmesan. The pasta dough that wraps around the filling is the kind you will find only in Piemonte, a lovely deep yellow that comes from the abundance of egg yolks in the recipe. The eggs here have nut-colored shells and are often harvested just days before they are used, but it is their bright reddish yolk that gives them such a decadently rich flavor.

What struck me most this morning was the lively energy in the room emanating from a group of mostly gray-haired, retired folks. There was talking, teasing, and joking, but they were also appropriately serious about the work at hand. One of the older ladies was at a table at the back of the room by herself, and I was told she was La

Maestra, the best of all of them. Her *plin* were indeed little works of art, perfectly formed and symmetrical, and she moved swiftly. She blushed when she was proclaimed La Maestra, but she did not deny it.

Another one of the women, in pearls and a leopard print sweater, told me she was the oldest one here. When I told her I didn't believe her, she said, yes, in fact she had just turned eighty-eight three days ago. I am pretty sure she was not the only octogenarian in the group. And every one of them was so kind to me. As busy as they were, each was happy to explain something, or show me their technique, and all were pleased to pose for any picture I wanted.

One of the ladies, around my age, asked me if I wanted to try my hand at it. I was honored to be asked, so of course I accepted, then painfully, slowly proceeded to make a few dozen frumpy, awkward little pouches. They had all made it look so easy. It wasn't.

As the morning progressed, with the laughter, the goodwill, and the warmth, I grew to realize that what makes Gemma so special isn't just the magic she forges from some flour, eggs (as extraordinary as they were), bits of meat, and vegetables. Her osteria is held together by love and pride and caring. She and her restaurant keep the little commune of Roddino thriving. On any given night, you will find one or two people, often alone, perhaps elderly, eating dinner at Da Gemma with her compliments, as her guest, completely free of charge. It may be the only hot meal they have all day.

Then, toward the end of my visit, I discovered something more, something that I had never known. As we were enjoying a coffee, Gemma told me how fortunate she felt to have friends like these, who come every Wednesday and work for hours to make the pasta for her osteria. In fact, she confided, these people do not work for money. They work here for the joy of it, for the pride they take in the finished product, and for the camaraderie. "They work here because they love me," she admitted. And none of them seemed to think this was out of the ordinary. It is what friends do. It is what builds a community, and in the end, a culture, one that sets Roddino, Monforte. and the Langhe apart from any place else that I have ever been. It is hard to imagine, in these divisive times, such pure kindness and generosity being the norm. While Americans are quick to help others in times of crisis, I feel like business as usual is often self-centered, focused on profit. I know that in my career I had been guilty of putting most of my energy into my company's accomplishments and the rewards that they brought. And I do not think I was alone. It is only very recently that American companies and individuals have begun to recognize the power of simply helping one another, with no quid pro quo. The business model of Osteria Da Gemma has always been like this.

Photos
Osteria Da Gemma

It is what I truly love about this region, this town. That and, well, the pasta.

CHAPTER TWO

L ike Alice tumbling down the rabbit hole, I chanced upon this
land at the end of March, five years ago. My husband, Kim, and
I were on vacation, our honeymoon, actually, and spring in Europe
was not yet fully awake. We had spent one idyllic week drinking in
the beauty and grandeur of Beaune, in Southern France, resplendent
with wines and the opulence of French food. Now it was time to
set off on the second half of our trip and head to the little town of
Monforte in Italy's Piemonte region.

For the first few hours, still driving through France, the weather
was mild and the scenery calming. But as we crossed over into Italy,
the roads became mostly frantic, confusing freeways, nondescript
highways that could have existed anywhere. The sky dulled and
developing clouds hung low, colorless against the flat landscape.
An early spring storm was threatening, the hours dragged on, and I
began to worry about what lay ahead.

Since I was the one who had lived and traveled in Europe for my
job, it naturally fell to me to find the places for my new husband and
me to stay. I had chosen the Hotel Villa Beccaris, based solely on the
website of the travel writer Karen Brown, who has always managed
to uncover for me little inns with charm, style, and character. Villa
Beccaris looked to have all of those traits. There were not many

photographs, but in the ones I did see, the property appeared splendid. Still, I knew nothing about the town, or much about the region; I picked it simply because visiting Italy sounded appealing, and this part of it was convenient to Geneva, where our trip began and would end. I could have just as easily thrown a dart at a map. Looking at our surroundings now, it occurred to me that I had not spent nearly enough time planning this part of our trip and a growing sense of dread began to gnaw at me. Perhaps I had made a big mistake; perhaps we would find ourselves in some dreary town with nothing to see or do. What an inauspicious end to our honeymoon that would be.

It was late afternoon and our GPS told us we were still an hour from Monforte when the gathering gloom turned to an icy rain. The unremarkable countryside on the outskirts of Turin looked monotonous, mostly industrial, and the silence in the car was broken only by the *flip-flap* of the windshield wipers. I began to notice a change in the terrain as we entered the area of Piemonte called the Langhe. Here, Italy became more agricultural. The factories and roadside bars were replaced by farms and stone houses; towns and church steeples began to crown the hilltops. But while the flat lands had become undulating and more interesting, the fog and rain obscured much of what we could see and, frankly, negotiating the winding roads required all of our attention.

Finally, with evening setting in, we left the main highway, made the turn up a long road, and saw the sign for Monforte. We climbed the twisting road for a few miles, ever upward. As soon as we leveled off and pulled into the town square, the GPS had us turn a sharp left up an impossibly narrow cobblestone street. *This couldn't be right*, I was thinking. Barely able to maneuver the tight turns, we went forward and back, up the steep hill, around and behind the town, teetering along the slick, muddy road. I had visions of us stranded on this lonely roadside all night.

At last, we saw a faded sign pointing to Hotel Villa Beccaris. Pulling off the uneven road onto a paved driveway and twisting around another few turns, we found ourselves facing the hotel entrance. The hotel appeared deserted. I stepped carefully out of the car onto the slippery pavers, found my way through the rain to reception, and there, waiting behind the desk, was the loveliest young woman.

"*Buongiorno?*" I said timidly, using nearly all of my Italian, and using it, by the way, incorrectly.

"Signora Boyle?" she asked, smiling. "*Buona sera.* You are here! Welcome to Villa Beccaris. Your room is ready for you. We have upgraded you to our nicest one. I hope you like it."

Even in English, I was speechless. How did she know my name? Why were we upgraded? And wow, was she pretty.

Her name was Monica, and I walked her outside to introduce her to my husband who had just managed to unfold his long body and climb out of the little rental car. As tired as he was, he looked down at Monica and smiled, and I could see he was as charmed as I was. Between the three of us, we assembled our suitcases, parked the car properly, and made our way through the courtyard and up the old, gracious, marble stairs to room 205.

The room had a high, domed ceiling painted with frescoes, two sets of French doors facing the gardens and pool, and two more windows facing south, each draped in rich blues and golds. There was a separate section in the back of the room to stash our luggage, clothes, and belongings. The room was furnished in Italian antiques, velvet chairs, and a wonderfully comfortable bed dressed in Frette linens. The bathroom was small, but chic, in white marble, and appointed with everything we could possibly need. I decided that even if the town proved to be uninspiring, I would be perfectly happy in this room for the next five days.

We unpacked, settled in, and started to unwind from the long drive. Soon feeling refreshed and somewhat cheered, we began to think about dinner. We dressed up a bit then went downstairs to reception to ask Monica if we could dine in the hotel. She explained that they serve breakfast and a light lunch, but unfortunately not dinner. We asked if she could then recommend somewhere nearby, a small restaurant where we could enjoy something simple and light.

"Actually, today is Tuesday so the town of Monforte is closed, which means most of the restaurants are closed, too. But there is one in town that is open, and I can reserve a table for you. Ristorante Da Felicin. It is down the hill, just a few kilometers away. You could walk."

This answer was a little confusing. Do entire towns close here? On Tuesdays? Would someone really walk down, much less back up that steep hill, in this weather? I looked out the door at the freezing rain and the slippery cobblestone streets. "All right. Thank you. But with this rain and my shoes . . . is there a taxi?"

"Yes, there is," she replied, "but he is in Milan."

This answer also stopped me for a minute. There was just one taxi? And how did she know where he was? Then she smiled her amazing smile, and said, "It is OK. I have my car. I will take you." She took her keys, locked up the hotel, brought her car around, and drove us to the restaurant.

When we arrived at Da Felicin, a sprawling, elegant albergo with white tablecloths, chandeliers, art, and flowers everywhere, we were the only ones in the restaurant. The chef and owner, Nino, came out to greet us in very good English, welcoming us as if we were old friends. He began by leading us down a marble stairway and gave us a tour of the wine cellar, which boasted an extensive collection of old Barolos and Barberas, as well as newer vintages, all from the Langhe region. Next, he led us up to the dining room, sat us at a table near the window, and asked us if we wanted a menu, or could he just bring us selections from the kitchen? If we like the dish, we eat it. If not, he would bring us something else, and so on until we were full. He asked us just to inform him of any food allergies or aversions, and he would do the rest.

Kim is a far bolder epicure than I am and readily agreed to try whatever Nino chose for him. I asked for something light, and the chef seemed pleased with both challenges. We ordered both a dry white wine and a delicious local red, and Nino brought us each different dishes and different courses for the next two hours. I had a beautiful salad with fresh, briny olive oil and a squirt of lemon, and a nicely roasted fish dressed with more olive oil, pine nuts, and a few briny olives. My husband devoured a series of antipasti and a plate of *carne cruda*, a kind of a veal carpaccio that we have since learned is a part of any proper Piemontese menu. When Kim finally announced that all he possibly still had room for was a small plate of pasta, the chef returned with a beautiful dish of tagliatelle, which he named *"Pasta Frigorifero.* Pasta ... with everything from the refrigerator on top!" I can only imagine what his refrigerator looked like compared to mine, because it was superb. The pasta was a rich saffron color, and tossed with a deep red tomato sauce, mellowed with both ground veal and pork. Between the wine, the setting, the amazing food, and the ambience, it was one of the most pleasant dinners I have ever eaten, and certainly one I will remember for a lifetime.

Over coffee, just as we were wondering how we would possibly get back up the hill to the hotel, Nino appeared with his car keys and proclaimed that he would drive us back to Hotel Villa Beccaris. After all, he had promised Monica that he would. On the ride home, my husband asked Nino if he could recommend somewhere we could go to taste the local wines. He immediately gave us the name of his friend Silvano Bolmida, who has a winery on the outskirts of Monforte, so we thanked him for that and, of course, for such a memorable evening.

That night, the pillows and sheets were so perfect, I was so comfortably full, and the night was so completely quiet that I slept like I hadn't slept since I was a young girl. In the early morning, still in a floating, dreamy state, I smelled the aroma of chocolate cake wafting up from the kitchen below us. It was enough to awaken some of my senses, but not enough to wake me, so I smiled and fell back to sleep for another hour. When I was finally ready to get out of bed, Kim remained curled up like a hibernating bear. I saw from our window that a light snow had fallen in the night, and was clinging to the grass and trees, but the streets were clear. In fact, the sky was a bright blue, so I quietly dressed in my walking shoes and down jacket and went downstairs for a cup of tea and my morning walk.

The warm chocolate torte had been placed on the table in the breakfast room, along with platters of other breakfast foods, but I decided to work up an appetite first. I finished my tea, then set out with great curiosity and a bounce to my step. The morning was new and freshly washed after the storm of the day before.

I went out through the old courtyard to the street and began walking down the hill. It was not nearly as foreboding as it had been the night before. I saw an ancient church and a lovely medieval town to the right, tumbling down the hill like stone and tile building blocks, a soft terra-cotta color in the morning light. Beyond the rooftops were rolling hills and fields of neat, snow-covered vineyards as far as the eye could see. Then something stopped me short. What was that in the distance? There were high craggy mountains piled with snow, just on the horizon. I was stunned. Could those be the Alps? I had no idea we were so near the Alps, much less surrounded by them. The vista in the crisp morning air literally took my breath away. I ran back into the hotel to wake up Kim and tell him. This morning was too beautiful to sleep through.

We made our way to the breakfast room, the *Limonaia*, a graceful structure made of iron and glass on all sides, including the roof. It is perched on a cliff on the far northern part of the hotel and looks out over the valleys from Monforte to Barolo and beyond. Little tables were placed all around the edges, so the effect was a bit like sitting in a bird's nest overlooking the world. The view was spectacular, and as I stood looking out the windows at the little farms and homes and wineries in the distance, I thought about the people who lived there. What a wonderful morning they must be having. What wonderful mornings they must have every day, drinking their coffee surrounded by the vineyards and the Alps and beautiful hazelnut orchards, which to them must seem so familiar and normal, but to me seemed slightly ethereal. I let myself fantasize for a moment that I was waking up in a home like that, a home of my own, in this magical part of Italy. Having allowed that image to burn into my brain, it was not an easy one to forget.

Meanwhile, and more pressingly, the breakfast was before me in all its glory. Calling to me from a long table in the center of the room were platters of various cheeses of different shapes, sizes, and colors, along with prosciuttos and ham, bowls of fresh yogurts, jams, honey, and rolls and breads, both sweet and savory, all for guests to help themselves. There were piles of pink and green apples, a chopped fruit salad, dried figs and apricots, nuts, cornflakes and house-made granola, sugared croissants, biscotti, rustic crumbles, and fancy tortes, including the chocolate one whose aroma I had already enjoyed. There was a giant pitcher of blood orange juice, deep red and sweet, and apple and grapefruit juices, as well. On one end was a rolling toaster contraption and a giant steaming pot of water with a timer that let you boil your own egg to your exact liking, or the chef would make you any other egg dish you could think of. All of this was presented on a white tablecloth, with silver serving dishes and fresh flowers.

Overwhelmed, I carried my little plate back and forth browsing the temptations, until a waiter in a smart black-and-white uniform asked for my beverage order: coffee, espresso, or any other kind of beverage I might want. It wasn't until I had finally filled my plate and sat down at our table that I realized we were the only guests in the hotel. This extravagant feast was just for the two of us.

And, as it turned out, the magnificent feast that is Monforte, the Langhe, and Piemonte was only beginning.

✳✳✳Torta al Cioccolato Villa Beccaris✳✳✳

3 cups flour
2 cups sugar
3 tablespoons cocoa powder
1 teaspoon salt
1½ tablespoons "lievito" (dry yeast) or baking powder
3 eggs
⅔ cup plain yogurt, whole
1 cup milk, whole or 2 percent
½ cup sunflower oil
8 ounces semisweet or dark chocolate mini-chips

Grease two round 8" or 9" cake pans and line with parchment paper.
Preheat oven to 325 degrees Fahrenheit.

Measure the flour, sugar, cocoa powder, salt, and dry yeast or baking
powder into a large bowl, and stir with a fork to combine. In another
bowl, add the eggs, yogurt, milk, and oil and beat well with a large
whisk. Pour the liquid mixture gently into the dry ingredients and
whisk well.

Spread the chocolate chips into a thin layer at the bottom of each baking
pan. Then, using a measuring cup, pour equal amounts of the batter
into each pan.

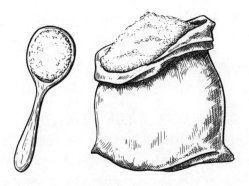

Bake at 325° F for 40 to 45 minutes or until a toothpick inserted into the center of each cake comes out clean. Let cool in the pan for 10 to 15 minutes. Then, placing a cookie sheet on top of the cake, quickly and carefully invert the cake pan upside down, and tap it to ensure that the cake falls out in one piece. Peel off the parchment paper from the bottom of the cake, then carefully invert the cake again onto your serving platter so that the melted chocolate is once again at the bottom of the cake. Sprinkle the top with powdered sugar if desired. Excellent when served warm or at room temperature with a dollop of whipped cream.

CHAPTER THREE

S liding deeper and deeper into this wonderland, I gave myself over to the charms of this decidedly different world, and in the next few days, Monforte and the Langhe began to engulf me.

The cobblestones in the piazza were pleasantly rough underfoot as we strolled from the cafe to the market, and back to the cafe, studying the various pastas and pastries for sale, and marveling at the medieval architecture soaring above in the old town. There were few tourists and we heard almost no English, pantomiming our needs and wishes to the amusement of the locals as we shopped. Then, at lunch, we received a text message from our new friend Nino confirming that he had organized a tour and tasting for us at Silvano Bolmida's vineyard for later that afternoon.

Maybe it was the weather, cool and romantic, maybe it was the gently rolling landscape filled with vineyards as far as the eye could see, or maybe it was the liquid ambrosia itself, but wine tasting here was unlike anything I had ever experienced before.

The tasting was to begin at three o'clock. We pulled into the driveway of the vineyard on time, but were greeted only by two growling, barking dogs. Everything felt off; perhaps we had the wrong address. There were no signs, no cellars or tasting rooms to be seen, no other cars and no reception at all. So we sat in the car, the

German shepherd drooling hungrily at me through my car window, and wondered what to do.

Then, from out of the mist in the vineyard, appeared a handsome, curly-haired man, graying at the temples, in dark blue jeans and a thick fleece jacket, striding toward us. There were clumps of mud still clinging to his boots from the fields and he was smiling from ear to ear. At his whistle, the two dogs backed away and curled up peacefully on the lawn.

I rolled down my window as he leaned in and said, "Welcome! You are here to taste wine, yes?"

"*Sì, per favore!*" I answered, using the final three words I knew in Italian.

He shook my hand enthusiastically. "By the way, I am Silvano."

He invited us into the old barn, which, as it turned out, housed a cozy tasting room and fronted his many barrels of freshly picked grape juice, happily fermenting its way to becoming wine.

"We will taste. But first, we relax. Would you like a coffee? A cigarette?" I politely declined, my husband took a coffee, and Silvano enjoyed both. He chatted amiably, in formidable English, asking about us, about where we were from, and how we were enjoying our visit. He then began to talk about his family, his vineyards, and his philosophy on making wine. There were no other tourists; it was just the three of us.

After a very agreeable half an hour, he said, "And now, let's taste!"

He led us up some narrow, wooden stairs into what had been the hayloft, and showed us his many barrels of wine. He told us he had studied nearby at the renowned Alba wine school, Scuola Enologica di Alba, even later teaching there, and had learned much about the science of winemaking. He explained how, through his own experimentation, he was discovering how to age his wine in oak long enough to get the rich flavor, but not so long that the tannins overwhelm the fruit.

Next, he brought out a wine thief, a long tube that allows him to reach into the various barrels and to taste the fermenting juices. Then he climbed up a ladder and opened the cap on the top of one of the casks. He slid the probe into the wine, siphoned it up, and poured each of us a taste of last year's vintage, right from the cask. It was intensely sweet and not yet wine-like, but far more interesting than grape juice. This was the juice of the famed Nebbiolo grapes that were growing right on the hillside above his farm, and all around the Langhe. As we sipped, Silvano explained what made Nebbiolo grapes so special. Nebbiolo grapes, if grown in precisely the right region, then aged for at least thirty-six months, twenty-four months of that in wood, and if their juice then passes a myriad of tests by officials representing the Denominazione di Origine Controllata e Garantita (DOCG), can earn the right to become a Barolo wine. And once the wine is called Barolo, it joins a family of wines heralded as among the best in the world, with a price tag to match.

"By the way, I know you have heard that Barolo is the king of wines, and the wine of kings. That is public relations talk. But it really is a beautiful wine, I think Italy's finest wine. Of course, maybe I am a little prejudiced."

I had not heard the "king of wines, wine of kings" phrase until that moment. But it is a line I have heard often since, referring to its popularity among nobility and the rulers of the House of Savoy years ago, and I think it is deserved. Of course, maybe I am a little prejudiced, too.

We had been enjoying Silvano for nearly two hours. He has the kind of easy charm that appeals to men as well as women, and both Kim and I were happy to sit back and listen to him explain the science, the art, the heritage of the wines he loves. But we were now beginning to smell some serious ragu aromas coming from next door. His mother and father live here, he explained, and mama was making supper. What I would have given to be invited to that meal!

"By the way," Silvano said finally, "I am sorry that this is taking so long—it is because I speak very, very slowly." He looked at us with a twinkle. "But now we need to taste the final product, and then my mother needs me to come for dinner."

We took a cursory tour of the bottling plant, which was simply the other side of the barn, where he selected six or seven bottles he wanted us to try.

As he poured, he spoke about each bottle's specific varietal and vintage, describing the weather for this and that year, the hot and dry year, the difficult rainy year. And he leaned out the window and pointed to different hills nearby to show us which bottle came from which particular vineyard. He owned ten rows from one hillside, forty from another, each one vastly different depending on which way the hill faced, how steep the slope was, and how old the vines were. Some of the wines we tasted were quite tannic, as many Barolos are, to my palate, but all had a lovely ruby color and a ripe fruit taste, and all were delicious. I love wine, and often enjoyed going wine tasting in California when I was younger. But never had anyone spent this amount of time and energy with me, and here the winemaker himself was sharing his time, his wisdom, and of course his wine, even as it was fermenting beside us.

It was now two and a half hours into our wine tasting, and we purchased a few bottles from Silvano to drink during our travels, one for a gift, and two to take home. He had spent nearly three hours with us, charged nothing for the tasting, and sold us only six bottles of wine.

But he gained lifelong admirers.

Warmed and sleepy from the wine, we drifted back to our room at Villa Beccaris and napped until it was dark. When we awoke, to my astonishment, I was hungry. Maybe I was still dreaming about Silvano's mother's ragu, but all the drinking and napping seemed to have worked up our appetites, so we went back down to the reception to ask about dinner. Monica was there, of course, with more suggestions. Once again, we asked for someplace with simple, light fare. She directed us into the old town, and told us we would find such a restaurant a few hundred meters down the road, on our right. The evening was chilly, but dry, and a walk sounded perfect.

We left the hotel and I slipped my arm into Kim's and walked for a ways in the dark, with only one amber-colored streetlight to show the way. There was a massive old villa and towering walls and buildings looming over either side of us. The winding pebbly street was empty, and steep enough that I had to watch my footing with each step, holding more tightly on to Kim for support. Just as we, once again, thought we had taken a wrong turn, we noticed a warm glow coming from a window up ahead on the right. We stopped and looked through the glass to see that inside was a well-lit room carved into the stone, filled with fashionably dressed people laughing, chatting, and drinking wine of every sort of vintage. They had a long buffet of hors d'oeuvres—free, of course—whole cheeses and sliced meats, nuts, grilled vegetables, frittatas and breads, with plates stacked up for you to serve yourself and stave off hunger while you savored your wine. There was a well-stocked bar, too, with a generously built, black-haired man behind it orchestrating the guests' wants and needs. He smiled as we walked in and immediately offered us a shot of grappa to tide us over until our table was ready.

The bartender was Giulio, owner of this establishment. His family is a legacy Monforte family who runs the town's only pharmacy. But the family business was not for him. He left it to his brother Paolo to manage and followed his own vision to create the magnificent and welcoming Case della Saracca, part wine bar, part restaurant and structural gem.

I had never in my life seen anything like it. In my world of neatly planned neighborhoods and strict building codes, Case della Saracca could not exist. It is actually five stories of glass and steel rooms carved into a block of homes from the oldest part of Monforte, cave-like houses over six hundred years old. The glass door opens to an expansive candlelit entry, while stone walls and wrought iron support the floors above. I clung to the iron railing with both hands as I climbed the steep, rocky steps to tables on the upper levels. The food is prepared in the kitchen on the fourth floor, and dining tables are precariously perched throughout from the first floor to the fifth, with spiraling steps, glass floors, and balconies interspersed along the way. One elevator carries hot food from floor to floor, but the servers climb up and down all night caring for patrons and serving guests, while maintaining very attractive physiques. There are dozens of candles flickering on tall metal posts on the entrance level, and if you walk a bit further, you find temperature-controlled rooms storing all sizes and shapes of cured meats and salamis, lit and hung behind glass like carnal art in a meat museum. Even the bathroom is one of those "you have to see the bathroom!" places. It, too, is carved into the stone, and as you wash your hands in the infinity sink, you can watch the water trickle out to the cave below it on the other side of the glass. The restaurant, and indeed the architectural achievement of it, is a wonder.

We found the food wonderful, as well. Being that it was a cold, wintry night, Giulio was offering the Piemontese specialty *bagna cauda* on the menu, which in the Piemontese dialect literally means hot bath. It is a kind of a fondue with whole vegetables that you dip into simmering hot olive oil doused with garlic and anchovies. It is a dish that shepherds and vineyard workers would take with them into the fields to warm and sustain them, and it did the same for us that night.

The next day I awoke and swore that I would never eat again. But after my walk, and during the delightful Villa Beccaris breakfast feast, we made plans for dinner. We asked Monica, now for the third time, to recommend a place for the evening that was simple and light. She immediately suggested Trattoria della Posta.

"It used to be the post office," she explained. Sounded simple to us. But, of course, it was not. It, too, was extraordinary. Set just out of town, a few minutes' drive away, the restaurant is an impeccably furnished home in the countryside, surrounded by lush, manicured gardens. Like virtually all of the other good restaurants here, it is owned and run by a local family, the Massolinos. Since 1875, the Massolino family and Marita and Gianfranco Massolino have helped define and refine Piemontese cuisine in their restaurant. They have created dishes that I now know and love and crave if I go for too long without: *ravioli del plin*, *carne cruda*, *vitello tonnato*, and local meats and wild game, roasted or braised to exquisite perfection.

That night, Kim and I drank a wonderful Barbaresco, and devoured focaccia bread that had an addictive, salty crunch. I had the best salad I think I have ever tasted—arugula and baby greens with warm, shredded capon, so lightly dressed with a sweet vinaigrette that it became one with the salad, then topped with a tiny poached egg that undoubtedly came from the same place as the capon. Kim chose the veal, infused with Barolo wine until it became beet colored, incredibly tender, and sweet. Then came the cheese course, which was a veritable landscape of cheeses. There were French, Swiss, and Italian selections, thirty of them or so, whose rinds resembled the aged stucco walls of Monforte's churches, and that tasted creamy and tangy, mild or robust, both fresh and aged. Kim chose three of them for dessert, but we both reminisced about the others long after our meal was finished.

For the rest of the week, every mouthful we ate, and every sip of wine we drank, was heavenly. And it seemed to me as if every person we encountered, whether they were man or woman, young or old and wrinkled, was beautiful, each in their own way, and kinder than they needed to be. When traveling before, whether for work or for myself, I noticed that, in many countries, people have an open ambivalence toward Americans, a mixture of respect for our finer accomplishments and disdain for the hubris we sometimes express. I will never forget a British colleague once telling me, after several drinks one night, how we Americans were "actually so very limited."

And I recall one afternoon in Paris being astounded, myself, by a group of rowdy Americans hooting and hollering at the table server, who shook her head and rolled her eyes as she walked away. But in this region, this little town, the people seemed to find my husband and me to be a novelty. They were patient, curious, and charming, embracing us unguardedly, without judgment. I felt truly welcome. I now know it is partly because of who the Italians are, and partly because the few Americans that have come here before us have been exceptionally gracious and good neighbors, and we have been the beneficiaries of their thoughtfulness.

What's more, I found the contrast between the rustic landscapes and the sophistication of the cuisine culture to be unique and startling. And the changing beauty of the landscape in the pink morning haze or late afternoon sunlight, even at the end of winter, was mesmerizing. The cumulative effect on me was a kind of euphoria and sense of well-being.

I did not know yet what we had stumbled onto, or through, but I knew we had found someplace special. And I knew that I wanted more.

Photos
Bella Monforte

✲✲✲*Silvano's Mama's Ragu*✲✲✲

Silvano's sister, Silvia, kindly shared with me her mother's, and now her own, recipe for ragu, which is actually not a recipe at all, but a philosophy:

Ragu is about family, culture, and love, to be handed down with care and treated seriously. Ragu is a passion. It should be very natural and never heavy-handed. Begin with an onion, finely chopped, sautéed slowly in a little olive oil, just a little oil. You don't want it to be heavy. You could use garlic instead of onion, but do not use both together because they have very different flavors and make each other bitter. (Silvia uses onion, and so did I.) Then, add lots of herbs, like fresh rosemary leaves pulled from the stem, parsley, oregano, either fresh or dried, or marjoram, all finely minced. Whatever you love. Cook the herbs with the onion for a few minutes, until the onion is translucent and golden, being careful not to brown. Add a few handfuls of roughly chopped celery and carrots for sweetness and cook all together for a little bit. Quanto basta. Just enough. Add a little bit of salt, but no pepper. Ever. Then add meat: about eight ounces of ground veal or pork, or, better yet, a combination of the two. Or you could use a good sausage, taken out of the sausage casing. Cook until the meat is just browned. "Ora, Il Segreto"; Now, The Secret. Add a small glass of red wine. Perhaps one of Silvano's wines. Cook until the wine evaporates and releases the alcohol. Next, add about ten ounces of tomatoes, either fresh and ripe from the garden or a good tomato sauce from a glass container, never a can. I use the tomatoes from my garden that I grow and put up in glass jars every summer to use for the rest of the year. San Marzano tomatoes are the best, if you can find them. Cook for a while over moderate heat, never high heat. For how long?

Abbastanza. Enough, not too much. It should taste fresh. The whole process should take only about an hour. When you are ready to serve, toss it with the cooked pasta, perhaps tajarin or tagliatelle, and top it all with a little bit of olive oil, fresh basil, and, of course, Parmesan.

❊❊❊Bagna Cauda❊❊❊

1 small head of garlic (about 2 ounces), separated and peeled
Milk
4 to 5 small anchovy filets, rinsed carefully and drained
½ cup of excellent olive oil

Mince all of the peeled garlic cloves, place in a small pot, and add milk to cover. Heat gently over very low heat for up to an hour, never allowing it to boil. This will help to mellow and sweeten the garlic flavor. Meanwhile, lightly chop the anchovies. Place the anchovies in a separate small pot and cover with the oil. Cook gently over low to medium heat, never allowing the mixture to boil, whisking occasionally, until the anchovies dissolve. Now drain the garlic, discarding the milk, and mash into a paste. Add the garlic paste to the anchovies and oil mixture. Place the warm mixture into a fondue-type pot over a low flame. Serve with a basket of vegetables for dipping, such as raw carrots, celery, cauliflower, cooked potatoes, and fennel. Bagna Cauda is also delicious served at room temperature as a sauce for grilled vegetables or atop bruschetta.

Trattoria della Posta Capon Salad with Egg

  1 capon or hen
  1 onion
  1 stalk of celery
  1 leek
  1 sprig of rosemary
  2 bay leaves
  2 basil leaves
  A few peppercorns, a few juniper berries, a piece of star anise
  Salt
  Assorted salad greens/vegetables
  Olive oil & balsamic vinegar
  Quail egg, if desired

Put the capon or hen in a large pot with plenty of water and add the onion, celery, leek, and herbs and spices. Bring to a boil, then simmer. Cook until the meat is tender, about 2 hours.

Prepare the salad, using a mix of various greens and vegetables like field salad and bitter greens, green beans, asparagus, cherry tomatoes, and red and yellow peppers. Cut all the vegetables into small pieces and arrange them attractively on a flat salad plate.

When the capon is cooked, remove it from the broth. After it is cool enough to handle, debone the capon and arrange small pieces of the meat on top of the salad.

Add salt, and drizzle with a vinaigrette of organic olive oil and balsamic vinegar reduction. At the last minute, top with a poached quail egg, well drained, if desired.

CHAPTER FOUR

Returning home to San Francisco, I realized I was smitten. Having fallen in love a few times in my life, I was familiar with the symptoms. Even though I was back to my perfectly pleasant life in America, I caught myself constantly thinking about Monforte, the rolling hills and the valleys stretching all the way out to the Alps, the lively piazza with its meandering cobblestone streets, and the innate appeal of its people. I would talk endlessly about Monforte to anyone who would listen, looking for excuses to bring up the subject, just so I could recount its many charms. I lingered over photos I had taken, each time finding something new to enjoy. At night, I would fall asleep imagining myself going about the day in one of the tile-roofed homes I had seen tucked in amongst Monforte's vineyards, and then I would dream.

But was this love? Or was it just infatuation? Was this unfamiliar place somewhere we could maybe call home, if only for holidays? I needed to find out. I needed to go back again as soon as possible.

As for Kim, he was more hesitant to commit. We had a nice apartment in San Francisco that was easy and comfortable. Did we really need another home? And if so, he wondered, were there not many other towns in Italy, just as appealing as Monforte, but maybe with an ocean view? Or maybe there were other attractive

Italian towns, closer to a lake, or to an international airport. Besides, Monforte would have to wait. We had our lives to live back in the United States.

And now that we were back home, those real lives took over. I think this happens often to people after a wonderful vacation. Fantasies that seem so possible in a faraway place look starkly different when faced with the realities of life. Friends and family and the rhythms of our day-to-day tasks once again consumed our energies. Owning a home in Italy was a wonderful dream, but not exactly practical. I had just retired from a career in advertising, but Kim was still working enough that living abroad would be out of the question.

So life returned to normal. Normal, that is, except for the fact that it was our first year of marriage. And even though it was not the first marriage for either of us, it still felt new, a time of a little adjusting, and a lot of joy. I felt as if I had pulled one over on the universe finding love so late in life, being well over fifty, and feeling like life was just beginning again for me.

I was also still in the early days of my retirement. For years, I had thrown myself into the mad world of advertising. It was all consuming, exciting, and often thrilling. As a global creative director, I had lived in New York, San Francisco, Paris, and Frankfurt, traveling pretty much everywhere. I was lucky to work with some very talented creatives from dozens of countries, other writers and directors and art directors who taught me about design, color, and the power and possibilities of a global idea or the difference that something as small as a well-chosen typeface can make. I had presented new business pitches with adrenaline pumping through my veins as I showed our ideas to potential new clients. And I became friends with clients who inspired me with their vision and challenged me with their expectations. I had bosses who opened doors and gave me wings. And at times I worked day-to-day with a few shallow, insecure, and downright mean people who would easily stab me in the back if it suited their agenda. Through it all, I learned what I was capable of achieving. It was highly satisfying. And at times very draining. When I finally decided to leave the advertising business, I met with my agency leaders, gave my notice, and then immediately contracted walking pneumonia, as if my body was finally able to just let go. I spent the last few months of work dragging myself across the finish line, and when I packed up and left New York, I knew I was done and that I had given it my all. I moved west to live with my then-boyfriend, Kim, and spent my days trying to regain my strength. Now, nearly a year into retirement, newly married, and home from our honeymoon, I was beginning to get my second wind.

This slightly intoxicating sense that my life was entering a fresh new phase had a compelling effect on me. Maybe now, anything really was possible. I was no longer working; I was free and unfettered. It had taken us two lifetimes and former marriages to meet. Kim arrived in my life with a family of three young boys, and I in his with only an unfulfilled dream of a family and an all-consuming career. It took another decade for us to live in the same state and under the same roof, and to finally decide to marry. Now, with Kim's sons in college, off on their own interesting paths, and my career winding down, our future was a blank canvas. Maybe now we could create a life that was uniquely ours. Maybe now would be the perfect time to listen to those little voices in my head and those flutters in my heart. Could I build a life beyond the one I had grown up with? Could I navigate another culture and feel at home there? Could Kim and I build something for the two of us?

Maybe, just maybe, this Italian dream could come true.

Holding on to that glimmer of hope, I enlisted in a continuing education Italian class at the local high school two afternoons a week. It was ultra basic, with just two other beginners and myself, but since the only Italian I knew was *buongiorno*, *per favore*, and whatever I had picked up from Starbucks (*Frappuccino*?), I was exactly where I needed to be. The classes lasted a couple of months, and all I really learned were greetings, how to count to one hundred, and some random infinitive verbs, but it was a start. I would walk to school with my school books on my hip bone, the way I did when I was in high school. And at night, I would dutifully write out my exercises in my notebook. When summer came, my Italian was still pretty incompetent, but I was undaunted. I had lived in France and Germany at different times earlier in my life, learning to speak French and German well enough to chat with locals. I was loving the new challenge of trying to learn Italian, however long it took.

At the same time, Kim found a website that would send us listings of houses for sale in Piemonte. We often spent evenings curled up on the couch looking at the homes. Many were in partial ruins, but most were beautifully situated and intriguing to think about. The prices were, by American standards, surprisingly affordable. And while the homes all needed work, it seemed like it was a project we might enjoy doing together, each of us bringing our different skills into play.

That Kim had spent his career as a real estate developer made this whole project feel less capricious to me. On our very first date he told me how, at the age of twenty-eight, he had built a house. Having passed the California bar, he put his law degree in a drawer, moved to Vancouver, and became a cook and deckhand on a tugboat, then went off to work on the pipeline in Prudhoe Bay. He took all the cash he had saved and bought a small plot of land in the Canadian Rockies, along with a paperback on how to build a house, some lumber, and some tools. He then built the house. By hand. Himself. Just like that. He spent the rest of his career developing real estate, always learning, putting together partnerships and finding investors, building other homes, condominiums, and office buildings. I had loved the excitement and creativity involved in fixing up the homes where I had lived, but he was a real professional. So we spent much of those early days of marriage looking at Italian properties online, and dreaming about what we might possibly someday do with them, together.

Again, just in case.

It wasn't until eighteen months later that we were able to visit Italy again. I lobbied for going directly back to Monforte for the allotted three weeks to look seriously at property. But Kim wanted to explore Liguria as an option, as it was on the sea and still in Northern Italy. And he wanted to tour Monferrato, a similarly lovely region with lots of hills and farms. We compromised, agreeing to first explore Liguria and Monferrato and end the visit in Piemonte, this time with our good friends Rob and Carolyn, curious to get their fresh perspective on this part of the world.

Rob and Carolyn stepped off the train looking every bit the capable travelers that they were. Dressed in blacks and tans, with two compact carry-ons by their sides, they greeted us with outstretched arms, hearty laughter, and hugs. Friends of Kim's since college days long ago, they had welcomed me into Kim's life with such spontaneous warmth, I often forget they were Kim's friends first. The only time I am reminded that I am the newcomer is when we play bridge, which the three of them do with easy familiarity and alacrity. I had never played in my life before meeting them and am decidedly not a natural. But Rob is a patient teacher and Carolyn is as sweet as she is forgiving, so I swallow my pride and try my best to keep up with the three of them. Wine helps.

Liguria was our first stop. Carolyn, forever the "A" student, had spent weeks researching places to stay and cities to visit. She had found us a large, comfortable vacation home just a short drive from the beach. There was a little medieval town within easy walking distance, and no shortage of good restaurants, cafes, and shops. The local people were charming (I am now convinced that all Italians are), and the ocean was beautiful. But something was missing. The beachside neighborhoods were overly developed and crowded, even in September. The architecture of the homes in the towns was uninspired, not old, not new. There was no there there, no piazza where everyone would congregate or town center to beckon us. It felt to me that the sole purpose of the area was tourism. There were the locals, and then there were the tourists. And we were definitely the tourists. It was a lovely week, of course, as we were with great friends and it was the Italian Riviera, after all, but the area did not feel like a place we could call home.

A week later, the four of us drove to Monferrato where Carolyn had discovered a rental home, a charming old one, full of character. It was situated in a tiny little village, off a peaceful street with groves of mature chestnut trees, a garden, and rambling paths. Every morning when I took my walk, the only sounds I heard were the birds and the bells of the nearby churches. The living room had a giant stone fireplace that we would light in the evenings as we grilled dinner, played cards, and chatted late into the night. In all, the home was welcoming and delightful. But there was no café or restaurant in the town near to where we were staying. And as we drove around the different nearby towns, we saw almost no one out and about.

So many of the little villages we visited throughout Monferrato were all shuttered and nearly abandoned. The churches sat empty. And the restaurants, which served very good food, seemed to be tucked away in isolated areas, not part of a thriving community. I saw one or two elderly people walking along the streets, but there was no sense of young families or the liveliness and energy they generate. I don't know, but I imagine that the young people who grew up in these towns had moved away to Milan or Rome, or maybe New York, in search of careers or opportunity. They certainly were not here opening businesses and making their homes.

I have since learned that this sense of emptiness is a real phenomenon in many parts of Italy, where hundreds of rural Italian villages have been nearly abandoned. A sad nexus of poverty, urbanization, mass emigration, and natural disasters has practically emptied many of these towns where houses and schools are vacant and fields turn to weeds. I have even read stories in American newspapers about small communities in Italy where the mayor is offering free or nearly free homes to people, just to bring in residents and visitors. In Piemonte, it is entirely different. The wine boom has bolstered the economy and the children who grow up there often return to launch their careers and raise families. It is true with Silvano Bolmida's children, and I have since become acquainted with many others. For me, it is part of what gives the Langhe such vibrancy and vitality.

Nonetheless, we had a wonderful trip with Rob and Carolyn in both Liguria and Monferrato. Whenever we came across a new little hill or beach town, we would discuss the merits of each among the four of us and try to imagine living there. One morning, Carolyn suggested we visit Casale, a little town she had read about that was known as the City of Flowers. It truly was bedecked in flowers everywhere, blooming inside public gardens and outside private homes, hanging in baskets along the streets, and in and around the castle, the palaces, and the churches. We stopped and ate lunch at a trattoria in a whitewashed little cottage that served traditional Piemontese cuisine. I ordered roast veal smothered in Barolo with vegetables, cooked for hours. It was so tender it fell apart at the touch of my fork. It was perfection.

Walking out of the restaurant after lunch, we noticed that it was connected to an old barn that had been converted into a grappa distillery. We saw trucks filled with grapes, all waiting in line, and we watched as the workers unloaded the bunches onto a conveyor belt. It fed into an old winepress that then transferred the juice into the giant still. The musty aroma beckoned us, so, of course, we had to stay and taste the final result. At first sip, it burned my mouth and tongue, then it melted into a sweet, grapey honey that slithered down my throat to my belly. It was such a strange and slightly painful pleasure, enough to make me consider the City of Flowers and Grappa as a place to live.

On another evening, we were fortunate enough to stumble onto and into Ristorante Da Maria, in the little *frazione* of Zanco, where we devoured another meal that is forever etched in my heart. We arrived early and were the only people in the restaurant. This happens often to me. Italians are happy to seat you at seven thirty, but no one really eats until at least eight, so they bring you bread-sticks and, if you insist, a glass of wine. Of course, we do insist, and we all drank our wine and looked at the menu and chatted with the two brothers and current owners, Giorgio and Roberto Penna, grandsons of the original chef, Maria, who founded the restaurant some one hundred years ago.

In their best English, the brothers informed us that there was to be only one other table that night, but that party was a group of their special friends. At the request of their friends, they had procured some fresh-caught shrimp from Liguria for the occasion and asked us if we wanted to taste some of that, too. Raw. Yes, we said, we certainly did. So, after they brought out some typical antipasti—sweet roasted peppers, spinach frittata, rosy *vitello* with creamy *tonnato* sauce, and then the *carne cruda*, the raw, chopped veal—the brothers brought us the special platter of raw, chopped shrimp drizzled with olive oil and just a spritz of lemon. Next came the various pastas, salads, and main courses like rabbit and more variations of veal.

Finally, we were offered chopped fruit and *dolce*, accompanied by grappa and coffee. As we tried to stand up from our chairs, the brothers came back out and invited us down to their wine cellar. Underneath the length of the restaurant was a cantina filled with dozens of local wines from vintages going back decades. I was happy just to walk a few meters and sip a *digestivo*, while we viewed a photo gallery of their parents and grandparents and listened to stories of how their grandmother started the restaurant a century ago. As we left, the one other table was still enjoying their celebratory meal, and we thanked them for letting us be a part of it. We left feeling like we, too, somehow had become special friends, if only for the evening.

The next day, Rob and Carolyn said farewell to us and began their journey back to the States, but my husband and I were not quite finished. This tour of Italy had been wonderful—we found charming people in each of the two regions, and some scenic old towns with much to offer. But after two weeks of exploring and some memorable experiences, I had not come across any place that quite captured my heart the way Monforte had.

Fortunately for Kim and me, the next and final stop on our itinerary was the Hotel Villa Beccaris in Monforte. As we drove the two hours north to Piemonte, I wondered if it would all be as magical as I remembered.

✽✽✽Veal Infused in Barolo✽✽✽

Good flaky salt
3 pounds of veal (or beef) shoulder, rump roast, or top round
2 tablespoons olive oil
1 tablespoon butter
3 carrots, cut into 1-inch chunks
2 stalks celery, sliced
1 onion, sliced
2 sprigs each of rosemary, thyme, and sage, a bay leaf, a few
    peppercorns, a few cloves plus one stick of cinnamon, all
    wrapped in cheesecloth and bundled with string
1–2 bottles of Barolo or Nebbiolo wine
2 cups veal or vegetable stock, or more as needed
¼ cup chopped parsley, for garnish

The day before serving: Sprinkle salt lightly all over the meat. Heat the olive oil and butter in a large sauté pan over medium-high heat. Carefully add the meat, browning it on all sides to seal in the juices. When nicely browned, remove the meat and place it in a large glass bowl. Let cool, then add the vegetables, the herb bundle, and wine and stock to cover. Cover the bowl with plastic wrap and chill in the refrigerator overnight, turning the meat occasionally.

Braising: The next day, place the meat along with the marinade into a heavy skillet or Dutch oven on top of the stove. Bring to a boil for a minute, then turn down the heat and simmer leisurely, over a very low flame, for 2½ to 3 hours. The meat will shrink to about half its size and be rather dark on the outside. Be sure to keep the meat nearly covered with liquid, adding more wine or stock if needed. The meat is ready when it is fall-apart tender.

To serve: Remove the meat from the skillet, place it along with the vegetables on a heated serving dish, and cover it with foil. Remove the herb packet, strain the marinade into a sauce pan, and bring it to a rapid boil, uncovered, until it is somewhat reduced. Meanwhile, slice or portion the meat and place the vegetables alongside. When the marinade is nicely thickened, serve it as a sauce over the sliced meat accompanied by boiled potatoes or polenta, and sprinkle all over with parsley. Serve with another bottle of Barolo or a good Nebbiolo.

CHAPTER FIVE

The drive up the curving road to Monforte was at once familiar yet new. The medieval church graced the very top of the hill, as it always had, and the rambling buildings and homes scattered along the way were still the same. But looking out over the valley, the boundless vineyards and hazelnut orchards had turned from green to the most vibrant golds, reds, and rusts, and the sky was the intense blue of late September, a decidedly different world from the one we had seen before in spring. The grapes were being harvested and some vines were stripped clean, but the ones that remained hung low, heavy, and purplish black, just begging to be plucked. Wine tractors rumbled along in front of us, pulling over where they could let us pass, and we waved a thank-you as we admired their cargo, red plastic bins overflowing with ripe, dark clusters of the fruit.

We headed up with some confidence now to the Hotel Villa Beccaris, taking the slightly longer but less death-defying route, down and around past the back of the town to the entrance of the hotel. Monica was again waiting for us with that smile of hers: "*Bentornati!*" She introduced us to her equally lovely colleague, Jessica, whose blond hair and blue eyes framed her own amazing smile. And we were given our same perfect room 205, where we dropped our suitcases, opened the drapes and the doors to the balcony, then stretched out on the bed. It felt like home. Home, that is, if you lived in a venerable old Italian villa.

Legend has it that the Villa Beccaris is where the Rolling Stones once stayed when they were touring in Italy, and with its cool elegance and ideal location, just outside of the town center surrounded by a walled garden, I believe it. I also like to imagine that they would have assigned Mick to our room 205. It certainly made me feel like a pampered star.

That night, we walked down the road to the old town to dine again at Case della Saracca where the candles flickered everywhere against the glass and stone. Even though this time I knew what to expect, I was struck again by the incongruity as well as the beauty of the sleek modern venue tucked into the weathered old walls. In the months since we first visited, it had been updated even further. Now there was an entire wall of stainless steel wine vats backlit with blue lights and outfitted with levers designed to produce a perfect single pour of dozens of good wines. This modern technology had not yet arrived in bars in New York or San Francisco. And maybe it was because it was a weeknight and the local twenty- and thirty-somethings had gravitated here after work to mingle and flirt, but that evening's clientele was as hip and well heeled as any I had seen in any of America's chic cities.

Giulio, as always, was holding forth behind the bar, but turned as we walked in and somehow remembered us.

"*Ciao*, Kim!" he bellowed and reached over the bar with his big hand and shook Kim's heartily, as if welcoming an old friend. "*Come va?*" he said, and smiled at me as well.

He turned back to the top shelf above the bar, pulled down a bottle of old grappa, and poured a shot for each of us, handing them to us without asking. I certainly did not want to be rude, so what could I do but accept? It had the most delicious sweet heat that warmed me inside. Then he showed us to a table for two in a quiet little room next to the bar with a view of his cellar, behind glass. Under romantic lighting, we peered at cases and cases of wine tucked in and around the stone. It was just the kind of spot to whet my appetite. We ordered wine, and I ordered a plate of roasted veal. My husband ordered *tajarin*, another local pasta we had become familiar with on our first visit. A kind of a narrow, hand-cut tagliatelle, *tajarin* has a rich golden color from the many egg yolks the Piemontese use in the pasta dough, and it was topped with a mellow ragu of minced pork and veal. We sipped a fresh Nebbiolo, and as we chatted, I felt that I had never been more relaxed and comfortable in my life, so at home.

I couldn't tell you which of us first broached the subject that night, but soon we were seriously discussing the possibility of buying a home in Monforte. We agreed it would be exciting to find something old and not expensive, something that needed to be restored. Since the first night we met, over ten years ago—a lifetime, really—we had spoken of such a thing. It was a dream we had each shared even before we had met one another—to live in Europe, in the countryside, and to renovate an old house to make it ours. We had discussed it for years. But by now, even I was getting bored with just listening to us talk about it. I felt it was time to actually do it, or to admit that we never would. We were married, I was retired, Kim was cutting back his work hours, and we were still young and healthy enough to take on an adventure like this. We had looked at homes in Piemonte online for eighteen months, and in our two visits to the area, we had already walked through several properties for sale. The prices of these dignified but falling-down old homes were modest. The time finally felt right, and now coming back to Monforte, so did the place.

We talked about the town itself, about how in Monforte's Piazza Umberto, really anything could be found: a place for a good meal and a glass of wine or a cappuccino (nine or ten places, as it turns out), a place to mail a letter or pay your electric bill, a pharmacy with someone to listen to your sore throat symptoms and offer you a remedy, and a gelateria with handmade gelato to further soothe the sore throat. If needed, you could buy accessories for your Harley-Davidson or Vespa, or visit the library, bakery, or hardware store. There was a bank, two grocery stores, two gift shops, a Red Cross office, the local police headquarters, a place to purchase the *International New York Times*, if you get there early enough in the morning, and, of course, a beautiful old Catholic church, even though Kim wasn't a Catholic and I was a very casual one. Regardless, we agreed it was a lively square, almost as if there was an intimate party going on there at any time, day or night, to which we were always invited.

There was the incomparable Barolo Bar where we first befriended the gracious Silvia, who greets us with a *"Benvenuti!"*, two kisses, and some wonderful wine and pasta. She recently became the proprietor of the old landmark pub and instantly turned it into the gathering place for locals and for Italians throughout the area. She exudes warmth and generosity. Once we complimented her on the homemade salami, so she sent an entire salami home with us as a gift. There is just nobody like Silvia.

Then there was the famous Grappolo D'Oro, at the heart of the little Piazza Umberto. It, too, is a touchstone for locals, the place to renew and refresh yourself, to warm up when you are cold, to cool off when you are hot, and to catch up on the essential gossip of the day. The Rinaldi family, Signor and Signora Rinaldi, Pier Paolo, Alberto, their families and the same servers are always to be found there. They run a lovely inn, a notable restaurant, and the town's mainstay for coffee, morning, noon, and night.

I said that I felt the more we became familiar with the town, the more I could see us living there. I loved the old church. I loved the old town. I could even find essential luxuries, like a manicure, and a car wash was just a minute's ride down the hill. This was not just a charming town for visitors, I realized. This would be an ideal place to create our life together.

✳✳✳ *Piemontese Egg Pasta Dough for Tajarin* ✳✳✳

1½ teaspoons good olive oil
2 large eggs plus 5 egg yolks
2 cups of organic flour, unsifted (type 00 flour)
1 teaspoon good, flaky salt
Small spray bottle filled with water

In a bowl, combine the oil and the eggs and beat together lightly. Set aside. In a second, medium bowl, add the flour and salt and stir lightly to incorporate. Then make a well in the center of the flour mixture. Now carefully pour the eggs and oil into the center of the well. Using your fingers, gradually begin to incorporate the liquid in the flour from the sides of the well, a little at a time. Finish by hand into a rough dough.

Using a bench scraper, remove the dough to an unfloured wooden board and immediately cover with plastic wrap since you never want the dough to dry out. Let it rest for 5 minutes. Uncover the dough and begin to knead, pushing with the heel of your palm, folding the dough over toward you, then turning it a quarter turn. Spray liberally with a water bottle to keep the dough pliable. Do not add more flour. It will be dry, but be patient; it will come together. Continue kneading with an easy rhythm for about 15 minutes. Shape the dough into a ball, quickly wrap it in plastic again, and let it rest for half an hour or more. It will keep several hours, or freeze well.

A few hours before serving, thaw the dough if necessary. Place into a pasta machine for rolling and cutting, following the directions from your machine. Allow the pasta to dry well before adding to a large pot of salted, boiling water. Drain.

Still, even after that night, and all the discussions and all the looking, the day I fell in love with my home caught me by surprise.

The owner of one of the cafes suggested a real estate agent, Mario, who picked us up at our hotel and spent the day with us, showing us apartments, as well as newer and older homes. Each was interesting in its own way, but none felt exactly right for us. At the end of our tour, we went back to his office, reviewed other listings, and began to really talk about the specifics of what we wanted. Talking was harder than you might think, since his English was far from perfect, and our Italian was only elementary, but with pictures, patience, and goodwill, we communicated. We wanted character and tranquility and were not afraid of a ruin. We wanted something older, and something big enough so friends and, importantly, our whole family could come visit and feel comfortable. I wanted birds, grass, mature trees, sun, and shade. My husband wanted a wine cellar.

Sitting in his office that afternoon, I felt a wave of excitement flow through me. Kim and I were able, with this awkward third party as witness, to finally spell out for ourselves just what we wanted, and discovered, amazingly, that we wanted almost exactly the same thing, with a tweak for him, and a tweak for me. For the first time, it all felt real.

But since we were heading back home in two days, we agreed with the agent that we would keep in touch by email and he agreed to continue to look. We planned to return in the spring, or maybe sooner if he found something perfect. We shook hands and went back to our hotel.

Early the next morning, the phone rang. It was Mario. During the night he remembered a property that might be completely wrong but could perhaps be interesting. If we wanted, he could take us there at two that day. The price was what we were hoping for, and the property sounded fairly large. The only problem I saw was that the home was not in the town of Monforte, but in Roddino. Roddino would barely qualify as a town. It is a *commune* that does not even appear on some maps of the area. Merely four hundred souls live there. It has one church, three good restaurants plus a pizza place, and a post office that is open three mornings a week. That is it. We had driven through Roddino a few times, and in the few seconds it takes to zip through town, I found it unremarkable. But my husband felt it was worth a quick look, so I reluctantly agreed to go along.

As it turned out, the home was not really even in Roddino, but outside of the *commune,* in Roddino's suburbs, as it were. We turned off the main road onto a long driveway that curled in front of a lovely big home. It was mostly brick, with a tile roof and dark green shutters. It had several mature trees, a big garden, and a staggering view out to the west.

"Is this it???" I asked, incredulous.

"No. It is that one there..." said Mario, pointing across the way to an old barn with a dilapidated pergola. "This newer one is where the sellers live. They are selling that old house and barn over there."

I turned and faced the empty old house and barn sitting demurely in the afternoon sun—tall, proud stone walls and rusted iron doors, broken windows and shutters, crowned with a roof of old terra-cotta tiles, logs, and twigs. There were two or three outbuildings, crammed with wood, wine barrels, old farm tools, wires, tiles, and stones. The house was situated precariously on a narrow level plain that sloped up the hill behind it and slid into the valley in front. And it looked out over the whole world—vineyards, hazelnut orchards, farms and forests, and even the little hill town of Monforte, all the way out to the craggy Alps, still brushed with just a smattering of snow on the highest peak.

I looked up at Kim who looked at me.

I touched him on the arm and said, "This is it."

"How can you say that?" he replied, always the pragmatist. "We haven't even seen it yet. Let's go take a look inside."

I do not remember much about what I saw inside the property that first afternoon, other than that it was huge, charming, rambling, and filled with spiders. There did not seem to be a real front door anywhere, and the actual house was rather small and sat behind the barn. The barn was massive, wet, muddy, and musty. Down a few stairs and to the back of the barn was a long, dank wine cellar that was knee deep in sludge and murky groundwater. This caught my husband's attention perhaps more than anything else about the house. The other rooms were a maze broken by a few stairs leading up, and a few more leading down, and a few leading nowhere. What I do remember very well is sitting on the grass overlooking the valley. Everyone else was exploring the house and I was alone, just the songs of a thousand birds calling from tree to tree and to me. The sun was warm and steady on my skin, but there was the barest of breezes. *This is it*, I thought again.

I was interrupted in my reverie by Mario. He informed me that the sellers had invited us for coffee on the terrace of their home. I now know that this is very much the custom; whether you are a potential buyer, an old friend, or a delivery person, any proper Piemontese will invite you for a coffee. And it is very rare, now, when I offer a coffee to a Piemontese visitor that they do not accept, sometimes taking it with sugar, but almost never with milk. I gratefully accepted a glass of water, my husband and Mario each enjoyed an espresso, and that was my first meeting with Biagio and Angela, two of the most delightful people I have ever known, and certainly the best neighbors on the planet.

Neither Biagio nor Angela speak English, but Biagio's smile says all he ever needs to say, and Angela seemed to understand whatever I tried to say to her. Fortunately, the really important words, like *caffe* and *vino* and *aqua*, are pretty international. But then Angela walked over to their impressive vegetable garden and picked a beautiful little flower, pale lavender colored with tear-shaped petals, and held it in the palm of her hand to show me. She said a word I didn't understand: *zafferano*. She plucked the intense crimson stigmas from the center of the blossom and gave the little threads to me to inspect. I thought, astonished, this was saffron. Then I remembered that the Milanese use saffron in their *Risotto alla Milanese* for the beautiful golden color and delicate flavor, and Milan is just a few hours away. Pleased that I understood the significance of her harvest, she went inside and returned with a small jar, placed more stigmas inside, and gave it to me. I would be delighted to break a few import laws to smuggle that precious gift back to San Francisco.

We made the offer on the house that night, uncharacteristically not negotiating the price, but we did add one large clause to the deal. Renovating this barn into a home was going to take some time, and many trips to Italy. As alluring as the Hotel Villa Beccaris was, it was certainly not within our budget for more than the occasional splurge. So, as part of our bargaining, we asked our agent to see if Biagio and Angela might have a spare room that we could rent from them when we came to visit. They told him they, in fact, did have a small apartment on the second floor of their home that they had built for Angela's father before he passed away. It had its own entrance, a small kitchen, a dining table, couch, and two twin beds that could be pushed together for couples. Serendipity. And with that, the deal was done.

The next day was a bureaucratic blur. Mario escorted us through the process of signing dozens of documents dozens of times, registering for a *codice fiscale* with the Italian government, which is a kind of social security number, then going to set up a local bank account and visiting a notary, returning to the house one more time, back and forth between Roddino, Monforte, and the larger town of Alba. There was one somewhat peculiar moment while we were driving along the road when Mario asked us if we were happy. Of course we were, we said. "Are you happy with my work?"

"Yes, very much so," we said. He was so kind to personally walk us through this process. He then explained that if we were happy, he would be able to continue on while we were in America and take care of the closing for us. It was customary that there would be a small fee for all of this work, work that would fall outside of the normal Realtor responsibilities. "Of course," we said again. "Will that be part of the closing costs?"

"No, it is separate, and usually paid directly to me, not through the company." We had never before heard of doing this in the United States, but we were in a different country, and that we well understood. The fee seemed a little high, three thousand euros, but we would simply not have been able to get the closing completed from San Francisco without help, for which we were grateful. So we agreed. We packed our bags that night and left for home the next day, somewhat in shock.

Settling into my seat on the plane to San Francisco, I had to pinch myself. I looked at Kim, and he looked at me.

"We have a home in Italy," Kim said and then we let that sink in. A beautiful old stone ruin, just waiting to be brought back to life. I could not stop smiling.

Photos
House at first sight

❊❊❊*Risotto alla Milanese*❊❊❊

8 cups of very good chicken broth (homemade if you have it,
*   since Italians say the secret to a great risotto is a great broth)*
30 threads, or "pistils," of saffron
2 tablespoons bone marrow from 3 or 4 beef bones (ask your
*   butcher for the kind used for Ossobuco, or for any bones rich*
*   in bone marrow)*
4 tablespoons butter, divided in two
1 small onion, finely chopped
2½ cups of Carnaroli rice
Salt and pepper to taste
1 cup of Parmigiano-Reggiano cheese, grated

Heat one cup of the broth until simmering, and add the saffron threads to allow them to soften and "bloom," releasing their intense yellow color. Set it aside while you prepare the rest of the dish. Heat the remaining broth in a medium pot and keep hot.

With a small knife, dig out the tender marrow from the bones until you have a generous 2 tablespoons. Add the marrow to a wide, straight-sided skillet or sauté pan, along with 2 tablespoons of the butter and the finely minced onion. Cook gently, stirring frequently, until the onion is transparent. On medium heat, add the rice and "toast" it until the mixture is shiny.

Now begin adding the hot broth to the mixture. Add one ladle to the rice, stirring until the liquid is absorbed. Add another ladle and stir until it is absorbed. Repeat this process over and over until the broth

is gone. This should take 15 minutes or more. Take your time. Save the reserved cup of yellow saffron broth to add in at the end. Finally, once the rice is done and all the liquid has been absorbed, and the rice is tender but ever so slightly al dente, remove from heat, add the remaining butter, salt, and pepper. Top with a few tablespoons of the grated cheese.

Cover the risotto and let it set for a minute or two, then transfer to heated serving dishes. Serve grated cheese alongside, but taste the dish before adding more cheese, since it is pretty perfect as it is and too much Parmesan could overwhelm the subtle flavors.

CHAPTER SIX

The whole next winter felt like the day after Christmas, with presents under the tree, unwrapped but still in their boxes waiting to be revisited and fully explored. Each morning I would wake up and remember that I have a home in Italy and could not wait to get out of bed. There was always something pressing to do, a flurry of phone calls to Italy to talk about our designs, logistics to coordinate, travel to plan, documents to notarize, lists to make, Italian to learn. At night, I would pull up the covers, close my eyes, and dream of falling asleep in my bed in Roddino, Italian stars twinkling down on me.

Wandering around this crazy, looming stone structure, I can feel my heart beating. On the ground floor, which still smells of animals, there is an unsteady wooden ladder leaning tentatively against the floor of the hayloft. Climbing the first few rungs, I find the space that will one day be my bedroom, covered in deep, wet hay. Looking up, I see a million stars, not through a skylight, but through the holes in the roof. The heavy wood beams are uneven and rugged as if dragged up straight from the forest floor and put in place. The stones in the walls that haven't crumbled away completely will need to be repointed and reinforced. I

try not to think about how many spiders and other creatures are living here. I wander out into the garden. It is a warm summer evening, and I picture sitting on our patio under the fig tree, chatting with friends and family, drinking Italian wine, having grilled something wonderful, listening to the birds, and watching the sun go down behind the distant Alps. I see fireflies leaving trails like comets as they flit across our meadow. And I imagine the day when I can ascend the steps up to our room, sliding into the welcome of my own crisp sheets, with the moon above illuminating the valleys that stretch for centuries before me.

With each passing day it became increasingly clear that realizing this dream of ours would not be a summer project. Nor a one-year project. Making a home out of our freshly purchased but uninhabitable barn was going to take patience. Unfortunately, patience is not a virtue I possess. At all. I would have liked to make a list, take it to someone who knows how to make roofs and walls and bathrooms, tell them to get started, then go buy a bed and some pillows and sheets and a new toilet seat and move in. Of course, this was not going to happen. I did not even know how to say roofs and walls and toilet seat in Italian. All of which made me slightly crazy. I was working hard trying to learn Italian, as best I could, when I could. In fact, I now knew how to say the days of the week. *Oggi e domenica*, for example. And next *martedì* I would study colors. Who knew when I would learn about toilets. These were all steps. Itty, bitty, *piccolo* steps. But steps, nonetheless.

Step One was to get a permit to change the barn into a structure for humans. The Italian government really does require that. There are homes for people, and homes for animals. We had one of each. But since we have no farm animals, just family and friends, getting permission to welcome them would be our first task. An agrarian community for many decades, people in the Langhe often live in simple homes attached to larger barns so their livestock is easy to access. The animals live on the ground floor, and the hay, both for insulation and for the animals' nourishment, is stored above them. Since beautiful vistas are literally everywhere you look, locals do not seem to prioritize the views when they build. The homes are created with thick stone walls and small but functional windows, easy to heat in the winter, and cool in the summer. It is simply practical. But it means that a good deal of the buildings have large, lofted rooms with glorious views, all designated for the horses, cows, and chickens. We wanted to enjoy the stunning panoramas the Piemontese take for granted, and that are surely under-appreciated by the animals. Once we were given permission, we would combine the barn and house, leaving the majority of the structure's integrity intact, while trying to find a way to create at least one large window looking out over the countryside.

I had fallen in love with the home's massive stone walls. To me, they are history and poetry. Part function, part sheer beauty. Lofty and rustic, they give the house the character we had dreamed of. They are a disorderly combination of Langhe stones and handmade terra-cotta bricks, held together with mud and mortar. Each single stone, some put in place three hundred years ago, for me represents the toil and dreams of generations before us. Our goal was to keep as many of them intact as possible, which meant that, in some places, we would need to blast off the stucco that had been plastered on for reinforcement over years, and in other spots, we would need to try and seamlessly patch over oddly shaped openings.

Maybe most of all, I loved the roof. It was a patchwork of weathered terra-cotta tiles, *coppas*, interspersed with old logs and branches. Looking up, you really could see the moon and stars and the Italian night in all its splendor. However, as romantic as it was, it obviously would not keep us warm and safe in our beds. We needed to find a way to maintain all that we loved about the roof and still keep out the rain and snow, bats and birds. Not an easy task.

As for the interior layout, that would take weeks and months and dozens of sketches to discover where three bedrooms, three baths, a living room, kitchen, and even the front door should be. The cantina, which was tucked under the old house and beside the barn, remained knee-deep in muck. My husband was determined to make it into an elegant room to entertain, to drink wine, and to serve dinner; I was too afraid of the spiders to even think about it, much less venture into it. Meanwhile, all of this required the technical expertise of skilled Italian locals, which we hoped we would find with Mario's help. Therefore, Step Two was to find our architect. And Step Three, the most important of all, was to find a builder. We quickly realized that these last two steps meant we once again needed to travel to Italy. Of course, I was thrilled at this news. Like I said, it was the day after Christmas, over and over again.

So, as soon as the snows melted, we returned to Monforte and Roddino, armed once again with Rob and Carolyn. They readily agreed to join us, curious to see the home we had finally settled on. They are quite knowledgeable about renovating homes, having redone several of their own homes over the years, and their love, support, and ideas were going to be invaluable. Their unstinting sense of humor wouldn't hurt either.

We met them on the road outside of Mille Luci, a lovely duplex apartment aptly named for the thousands of lights that grace the distant horizon. Of course, it was Carolyn, the perfect travel companion, who found it, amazingly located just a few kilometers from our property in Roddino. As soon as we arrived, we dropped our bags and drove over to our home that used to be for animals, to lay eyes on it for the first time since the closing. It was surrounded in green grass, far greener than what we had seen in the fall. And here and there were proud red tulips sprouting up, as if to say, "I have been cultivated before, and I will be again. Just you wait." The smell of the freshly cut lawn from Biagio and Angela's house filled the air, but the only sounds were the occasional barking of a dog and the lilting songs of bird after bird. It was as I remembered it, only better.

At Mille Luci, we had the downstairs unit, and Carolyn and Rob were upstairs. During the day, we would drive over to our property and tramp around, looking, measuring, and pondering the possibilities. We ate out some nights, and cooked at home some nights, taking turns at each other's places. After dinner, we played bridge, and then said good night. I normally slipped off to bed, and the next morning, my husband, Rob, and Carolyn would appear at breakfast with multiple new floor plan sketches they had drafted late into the evening. It became a routine. Each morning, I took part in the discussions of the merits of each plan. But they did the heavy lifting, the measuring of the elevations, the calculating of the topography for the parking and entrances, the designing of the foundation, heating, and electrical. I was, admittedly, out of my league.

I helped a little bit by trying out my Italian. And I mean, a very little bit. But I had made some progress over the winter after taking classes on Tuesday nights at the formidable Istituto Italiano Scuola in San Francisco. I also logged on to Duolingo when I had time, which seemed to be almost never. And there were orange stickies all over the house with the Italian names for things on them, so when I needed a bathtub, I would know to ask for *una vasca da bagno*. I felt like I was starting to understand a few more words and phrases, but usually when I opened my mouth to say something, nothing came out. It was humbling and frustrating. Fortunately, there were a few words I had down cold. Seven, to be exact. And as I was able to use all seven of them that week, I felt pretty darn good about myself. Here they are:

1. *La macchina*: Literally, the machine, this also translates to the car. Obviously, this is a very important word when you are traveling around looking at homes in the Italian countryside.

2. *Mio marito*: Another very important word, this is the person who was kind enough to drive *la macchina* all over creation, also known as my husband.

3. *Cattivo*: This is an excellent word. Google translates it as naughty, and in class we learned it as a word to describe terrible weather, or something evil.

I had the good fortune to use all three in an exchange with the stooped octogenarian who lived across the street from Mille Luci. We were having a bit of a hard time getting out of our driveway and onto the wet, narrow road one morning and found ourselves sliding down her grassy hill toward her barn. No farm animals were harmed, but we flattened some grass and dislodged a large stone before gunning it back up the hill and onto the road. The next morning this tiny, weathered old woman approached me on my walk and I was foolish enough to say "*Buongiorno*," which, incredibly, prompted her to begin speaking to me. Rapidly. I had no idea what she was saying but she was pointing to the tracks and the newly replaced rock and then muttered, "*Cattivo*." I don't know if she was referring to the trespasser or the weather, but I nodded and pointed to our car: "*La macchina . . . mio marito.*" "*Si, si.*" She smiled. "*Mio marito . . . cattivo!*" said I, throwing my husband under the proverbial bus. She seemed pleased with my confession and happily went on about her day, as did I.

4. *La carta*: I learned this word from Rosetta Stone. It means paper. And when you are working on plans for renovating a home, you go through a lot of it. We came equipped with a few tablets, but our sweet friends must have drawn up three or four floor plans a night, and my husband was going through almost as much by himself. Plus, we were getting to the point where we needed graph paper and transparent tracing paper, to fine-tune the plans. So we headed into town one morning in search of some transparent tracing paper.

The task seemed fairly daunting. But I couldn't believe it when I spotted the sign: *Cartoleria*. Yep, it was a stationary store tucked away from the main square, filled with tracing paper, graph paper, and any other kind of paper we might have wanted. I felt like I had won the lottery.

5. *Quindi*: So, *quindici* means fifteen, which is a word I felt pretty confident about. But every time we met with another architect or builder, they used the word *quindi*, over and over, at which point the person translating for us would stop, and not translate the word. I was getting pretty confused. I wondered if it was a slang word for fifteen, and why everything we were talking about took fifteen days, or was fifteen meters, or cost fifteen euros, and why no one was translating that for us. Turns out, it simply means so, or as Google says, then or therefore. I must have heard it *quindici* times a day. But now I know it.

6. *Il tulipano*: Really. This is the best way to learn a language. I will never forget that the word for that beautiful red flower blooming courageously in our yard is *il tulipano*. And now, neither will you.

7. *La tettoia*: Actually, my husband learned this one before I did. He kept pointing to the overhang above our porch and the architect would nod, and say, *tettoia*. And they used *tettoia* when we pointed to the eaves out back, and they used *tettoia* when we pointed to the canopy by the bedroom and the shed out back. *Quindi* . . . we know exactly where our *tettoie* are and what they look like. We just don't really know what the word for all of that is in English.

It was a start.

I also willingly helped out in the cooking and eating arena. I have been
an enthusiastic amateur cook ever since I first learned to make beef
stew as a Girl Scout. When I lived in Paris, I took a one-week Regional
French Cuisine class at Le Cordon Bleu. And I later completed a sev-
en-month professional course at the Institute of Culinary Education in
Manhattan with dreams of opening my own catering company one day,
but in the end, advertising prevailed. So, to me, the chance to experience Italian cuisine every day and begin to learn its secrets was exciting.

We had, at this point, become well acquainted with the
beloved *ravioli del plin*. These little pillows of heaven are made with
the classic pasta dough ubiquitous in the Langhe, the one that is
a rich golden color from the abundance of egg yolks called for in
the recipe. But what gives this pasta its magic is the *plin*, or pinch,
itself—that is key to the technique for creating each little bite. They
create pockets that are perfect for holding sauce, butter, or Parmesan
cheese, the way the nooks and crannies of an English muffin hold
the butter and jam. I think the best sauce for the *plin* is the simplest,
Burro e Salvia, butter and sage. The butter should never be browned
or fussed with in any way, just barely melted, and the sage is always
fresh from the garden and thrown in whole, or roughly chopped, just
a few fragrant leaves. That is it. The sauce is lightly tossed with the
ravioli and served with grated Parmesan. Not yet having mastered
making the ravioli from scratch, I found a few good pasta shops that
sold fresh-made *plin*. I would take them home, boil them until they
floated, then strain and sauce them. I served them for dinner with
a large mixed green salad and hot bread and we washed it all down
with Italian wine. I am no Marcella Hazan, but I made sure the four
of us were well nourished and happy all week.

Sitting around our dining room table at Mille Luci, work on
the floor plans for the house proceeded with vigor and creativity, late
at night and throughout the day. With each visit to our barn, Kim
and Rob measured and re-measured where the various stairs might
go throughout the house, making sure the steps were long enough

to accommodate my husband's long feet, and shallow enough to accommodate his creaky knees. Together, we discovered the only good solution for where the front door should go, and Kim and Rob somehow sorted out the engineering puzzle of where to park our car, creating thirty-eight stone steps from the parking area down to our front door in the process. Carolyn ingeniously solved the irksome problem of where to place the kitchen by suggesting we add a small new section off the living room, which is actually how the Piemontese used to do it, adding a small *cucinino* alongside their living rooms. And at our son Flynn's suggestion, we all agreed to take advantage of our west-facing view of the valleys and Alps by creating one large window in the living room, with doors that open to the terrace.

But in many ways, the house told us where to build. The home's basic footprint was the footprint, and by law we were not allowed to change it more than 10 percent, even if we had wanted to. And there were only so many places that the three bedrooms would work. So, in their wisdom, the design team—Kim, Rob, and Carolyn— worked out the perfect layout for our home and readied it for an architect, or geometra, and our team of builders, electricians, and plumbers to execute.

On the last night of Rob and Carolyn's visit, we bought a plastic table and four chairs from the supermarket. We then went to the butcher and ordered piles of prosciutto, salami, cheeses, and fruits, a couple of beers and some more wine. Then we all set up a picnic in front of our new home, in the weeds right in front of the old rusted barn door. It was a little bit chilly that early spring night, but what I remember is the warming laughter of great friends, great food, and a dream starting to come true.

The next morning we hugged our friends goodbye, checked out of Mille Luci, and ventured forth into a new dimension of our travels, moving into the little apartment at Biagio and Angela's house, which we now dubbed Casa Piccola.

Ravioli del Plin con Burro e Salvia

Filling for ravioli:
1 *medium onion, sliced*
1 *large carrot, sliced*
1 *sprig rosemary, leaves stripped and chopped*
½ *cup chicken stock*
2 *cups white wine*
1½ *pounds of cooked mixed meats, a nice blend, such as leftover*
   veal or pork roasts—the Italians often use rabbit, but we
   could use turkey, or simply cooked ground veal and pork
½ *cup grated Parmesan cheese*
1 *pound frozen chopped spinach, thawed*
3 *large eggs, plus 2 additional egg yolks, lightly beaten*
Salt
Freshly ground pepper
Dash of freshly grated nutmeg
Fresh sage leaves, butter, and Parmesan as needed for the
   Burro e Salvia sauce.

In a saucepan on the stove, add the onion, carrot, and rosemary and cover with chicken stock and wine. Bring to a boil, then reduce it to a gentle simmer. Braise until the vegetables are tender. Strain the vegetables, removing them from the liquids. When cool, combine the cooked vegetables with the meats and finely mince in a food processor or by hand. Then add Parmesan cheese, drained spinach, and beaten eggs. Add salt and pepper and chill until ready to use.

Making the ravioli del plin:
Using the recipe for Piemontese Egg Pasta Dough for Tajarin, roll out the sheets to their narrowest setting on the pasta machine. They will

be very thin and long, about 5 inches wide and 2 feet long. Take one long ribbon of dough and place it on a lightly floured wooden board lengthwise before you. Put a row of the filling in little mounds, a scant teaspoon each, about ¾ inch apart. Fold the top half of the dough toward you, over the filling. Press gently and firmly around the mounds and between them to prevent air pockets from forming when they cook. Repeat with remaining dough and filling. Next, take a scalloped ravioli cutter and run it along the length of the folded dough next to the bumps so that the two overlapping pieces of dough are sealed together in a strip. They will look like long, bumpy snakes. Then, with a quick flick of your wrist, separate the little mounds of filling, letting the dough curl up a little on the edges of each ravioli as you flick. Place the ravioli on a cookie sheet, cover with a cotton cloth, and refrigerate or freeze. Save any leftover bits of dough and keep covered, to roll out and reuse for more ravioli.

When ready to cook, bring a large pot of salted water to a boil. Add the ravioli and cook until al dente, about 5 minutes. In a deep skillet on low heat, melt a stick of butter and add several fresh sage leaves, chopped. Using a large slotted spoon, scoop the ravioli into the skillet, heat a few minutes in the butter and sage, add a large handful of Parmesan cheese, and toss well to coat. Serve in heated pasta bowls and pass more Parmesan.

CHAPTER SEVEN

Life at Casa Piccola had its own unique charms. It is a cozy home a stone's throw away from the construction taking place at our real home and was always ready for us if we came to visit for a week, for a month, or for several months. We had our privacy, and at the same time we enjoyed the security and companionship of Biagio and Angela who always took time in their day to show us the ways of life in the Langhe.

When we arrived, there was an awkward moment of exchanging keys, gesturing, each person smiling and hoping the other person understood what the other person was saying. Opening the door to the apartment, I was struck by how impeccably clean it was. And it was stocked with piles of sorbet-colored towels and plain white sheets, pillows and blankets, and perhaps twenty perfectly ironed, gaily printed cotton tablecloths with matching cloth napkins, more than I would ever use in a lifetime. But when I opened the kitchen cupboard, I felt a surge of tenderness, that feeling I felt as an adult whenever I walked back into my parents' home. Angela had equipped the tiny kitchen with coffee, hot chocolate, tea, milk, waters (still and sparkling, of course), olive oil, and condiments, along with various soups, rice, and basic pastas. There were two single beds, which she had pushed together into a *matrimoniale* bed for the two of us, an old wooden armoire for our clothes, a bathroom including a shower and a bidet (which I still do not really know how to use or why), a small couch, and a kitchen table with three chairs. Along one wall was a refrigerator, a small sink, an oven, and four electric burners, all laid out as efficiently as a ship's kitchen. It was just exactly all that we needed, and I felt immediately overwhelmed with gratitude.

That first day, as we were still unpacking, we heard a knock on the door. There stood Angela and Biagio with a bouquet of tulips and a small handful of early asparagus from their garden. Handshakes, a mingling of English and Italian words, and all the appropriate thank-yous and welcomes were attended to, with smiles all around, especially on me. That night I poached the tender asparagus in the sauté pan that Angela had provided for us. At the last minute I threw in baby peas, butter, and chopped, fresh mint. It tasted like spring.

I loved the view from our beds. I awoke each day and as I lifted my head from my pillow, I could look straight out through two lace curtain-draped windows across the neighbors' fields to the Alps and Monte Rosa, the graceful mountain that towers over the other Alps just beyond Milan. And from our living room we had two more windows that looked out over another equally fascinating view: our construction site. Now when we needed to meet with a builder, engineer, or architect, we could just run down the outside stairs, stride past Biagio's vegetable garden onto our property, and we were there. It meant we could work on the house throughout the day, and I had a clean, dry place to come back to and warm up, with the makings for coffee, lunch, and even a proper ladies' room at my disposal. These things are not unimportant when you have workmen on-site from dawn until dusk all day sharing one rudimentary outhouse.

Living in Casa Piccola, I developed new and soothing rhythms to my day. I found that if I resisted the urge to sleep in and rose early to drink my tea and eat breakfast, I had time for a lovely walk before we needed to be anywhere. But if I didn't come back from my walk and immediately wash and dry the dishes, I was out of whack for the whole day. It had been years since I did dishes each day by hand, without an automatic dishwasher, and I found that the cascading bubbles in the soapy water, the sponging down of mugs and plates, the satisfying rinsing in the hottest water I could stand, and the neat stacking of the dishes in the rack made me feel that I had accomplished something useful, even before 9:00 a.m. It became something of a Zen routine for me.

I rediscovered the sense of pride that came from scrubbing my own floors, sweeping my porch, and hanging out our wet clothes to dry until they were crisp, almost crunchy, before folding them neatly in stacks. It brought back memories of my mother with clothespins in her mouth, stretching up on tiptoe to hang up bedsheets in the California sun, or sponge mopping our linoleum floors, usually while singing along to the radio. These are things I had learned to do when I was very young, but I had long since forgotten the calming effect of such simple but important daily chores. With my career came the luxury of automatic washers and dryers, and even housekeepers and laundry services. It is funny to be reminded now of these activities as the pleasures that they are.

Dinners at Casa Piccola were also simple but delicious and, to me, rather romantic. Sometimes I would just cook up fresh pasta from the little market in town, and serve it with a big green salad, or oven roast a pork loin from the *macelleria* in a pan tossed with sliced apples and potatoes. The compact oven would get so nice and hot that everything cooked quickly and browned beautifully, and went so well with an ice-cold glass of Arneis, the dry, fresh white wine I found at the store for four euros, and which continues to be one of the pure pleasures of my life in Italy. Kim and I would sit at the little table in our kitchen/living room, always by candlelight, and talk about our day and what we needed to accomplish tomorrow. Then we would wash, dry, and put away all the dishes so we would have a clean, fresh start for the morning. I soon found I nearly always went to bed tired, and, in the deep, deep quiet of the countryside, slept soundly.

It was during that first week, while we were just settling into life in Italy at Casa Piccola, that we found the person who would most shape the final outcome of our home. Our builder, Zef.

We were in one of our first meetings with the firm that would be doing our final plans and blueprints and overseeing construction. It was a group recommended by our agent, Mario, who had evolved into a project manager role for us. The firm he had found was not made up of architects; they were geometras, and their expertise is to execute our ideas and make certain they are viable. The cost of a good geometra amounts to about a third of what an architect would charge, and in our situation, they were ideal. Much of the house was a given, and the location for many of the rooms was obvious. Still, there were various options and choices to be made, and in our meeting, as we debated the possibilities, there was a sudden palpable tension. We realized that, no matter what we agreed to here, all of it could change once actual construction began, and the question of who would bear the cost of these changes hung in the air. After all, it is impossible to predict what we might encounter as we deconstruct a three-hundred-year-old edifice created for both humans and animals, made of crumbling rocks and old timber, and perched on the side of a hill. With so many unanswered and unanswerable questions before us, the conversation was starting to become tense and uncomfortable. That is when Zef walked into our meeting and into our life.

He was dressed in clean, pressed work pants, a collared shirt, and a smart down vest. Mario introduced us, explaining that Zef had been building homes in and around the area for many years, and should certainly be someone we could ask to bid our project.

He spoke no English but extended his big hand to my husband and then to me, saying "*Piacere.*" He had a broad, open face, a square build that made him seem taller than he is, and his smile was kind and easy. Our agent described our project to him in Italian, and with his broken English translated Zef's comments and questions back to us. Even in the linguistic awkwardness, Zef was clearly thoughtful, professional, and respectful and I found myself hoping he would present the best bid. As soon as Zef arrived, the tensions eased, as he offered ideas and suggestions that immediately made sense.

After the meeting, we piled into our car with Zef and Mario and took a tour of several homes and restaurants that Zef had built or was building. His work with old stone houses was stunning, one project after the other. His new walls were indistinguishable from the old walls in the same home. They were all beautiful, and formidable in size and integrity. My husband and I agreed that his work was consistently outstanding, and sometimes truly remarkable.

Oddly, I found Zef's Italian easier to understand than that of any other local I had met. It turns out that was because he is not even Italian. He is an immigrant like us, only he came to Italy from Albania. He spoke Italian simply and clearly like someone who had learned it as a second language in school. Besides, his smile and his actions communicated as much as his words. Importantly, if someone was going to come into our lives and try to bring shape to our dreams, it needed to be someone we liked having around day in and day out. Someone like Zef.

The day we officially awarded the job to Zef, he appeared at the door to Casa Piccola with two cases of wine, a lovely Nebbiolo and a sweet dessert wine, a Moscato. We invited him in, and he accepted, sitting with us at the kitchen table as we opened the Nebbiolo and drank from chunky water glasses. We chatted for an hour or so, although in what language, I can't say. It didn't matter. We understood one another that evening, and have ever since.

Zef was kind, gracious, polite, and extraordinarily talented—selecting him was perhaps the best single decision we made in the whole building process. He listened to us, argued with us, advised us, and laughed with us from day one. It became a relationship we would always treasure, one that is in stark contrast to another relationship we had that would ultimately prove to be based on deception and knavery.

CHAPTER EIGHT

W hen beginning to renovate a home, start with the roof.
It certainly wasn't intuitive. Everything I had ever accomplished in life started from the ground up. But this is the way Zef said to do it. It is the way it is done here. We are decidedly the foreigners, stumbling over the language, learning new customs and traditions, touched by the grace and humble elegance of the people. So, we listened. We tried to understand their words and their wisdom. If they say we should start with the roof, we will start with the roof. Who were we to question people who make beautiful villas and castles that last for centuries? So we signed a contract with Zef for the roof, but only the roof, entitled *Segnalazione certificata di inizio attività per lavori di manutenzione straordinaria del tetto*, filled with more signatures than I could count. Unlike in America, a home is contracted and built one step at a time, *piano piano*. And it was what we commenced doing one cold autumn morning, with the snow-splattered faraway Alps as our backdrop.

It was early and the quiet seemed quieter. Even the voices in my head whispered. There were birds. And the rustling of the leaves. An occasional dog barking. Otherwise, it was heartpoundingly still.

Then we began, disrupting the silence, taking apart the toppling pile of stones and sticks, rock by rock. As we worked, the church bells from nearby Santa Margherita chimed seven, and then played a longer tune, just to be certain everyone was awake. In Italy, the bells signal every hour, but are more emphatic when it is time to work or go to school, eat lunch, eat dinner, or go to Sunday Mass. The Piemontese people work hard. They start early, take a nice long lunch and maybe a quick nap, and then work very late, sometimes past eight. And the work they do is not easy. Because the land is stippled with farms and vineyards, the tasks are very physical, tending the vines, gathering hay, digging, planting. Even just walking to work is harder than in cities back home. There is very little level ground, and the streets are often made of dirt or cobblestone, challenging every ankle, every step.

Zef and his crew, all Albanians, work like the Piemontese. They arrive on time, and immediately begin lifting and pounding. My husband and I slogged through the mud with them for the first hour or so, our boots caked with the sticky clay, watching and talking with Zef while they worked. In an hour, I was fatigued. The men laughed and bantered among themselves, but continued working until well past noon, and then drove off to a nearby trattoria for a *pranzo lavoratori*, a worker's lunch. For ten euros, they could enjoy an appetizer, pasta, a hot entrée (maybe roast pork or veal), dessert, wine, and coffee. Lunches like these are offered all over Italy to workers, although how the restaurants can make a profit, I cannot imagine. My husband and I, thankfully, escaped back to Casa Piccola, and after throwing my impossibly muddy boots into the garbage, I made a sandwich and took a nap. It is exhausting watching all that work. Two hours later, Zef and his men were back on-site, lifting and pounding again until it was too dark to see.

Zef's plan was to dismantle the roof, keeping aside the beautifully weathered terra-cotta tiles, *coppas*, to be put back again once the roof beams were in. But first, they were to build a cement collar around the top of each of the stone walls to hold them all together so that they don't collapse, which is a precarious task. If the walls do not cave in, they could set timbered beams in place and finally replace the original tiles on top. The aim was to have everything completed before the snows arrived in earnest, which was just a month or two away.

For the next few weeks while Zef took our roof apart, we continued to enjoy the homey comfort of Casa Piccola. And life there was sweet. One evening after dinner, we heard a knock at the door. There stood Biagio on our terrace in the dark. He was explaining something quickly to us, which we could not at all understand, finally urging us to follow him down the stairs to his and Angela's home. We followed dutifully, not having any idea what we were doing.

When we arrived, we saw before us a colorful spread of biscotti, cookies, sweets, and slices of cake. There were little cups and an espresso pot, small stemmed glasses, and a bottle of sparkling wine on the table. Angela finally brought out the Italian/English dictionary and read us the translation of the word "*compleanno*," birthday. It was Biagio's birthday, and they had invited us into their home to celebrate with him. There was a little more joyful confusion that followed as Kim and I tried to explain that the next day was also my birthday. Once all that was cleared up, we sat at their dining table before the exuberant fire and ate biscotti and drank bubbly wine and laughed and conversed for nearly an hour.

Biagio and my husband seem to have the ability to talk together for hours, even though neither one of them speaks a word of the other's language. I believe there is something in the language of goodwill and kindness that is universal. And I think there is something about the essential Italian dining table that fosters it. At the center of every Italian home, large or small, is the long wooden table with chairs for family members and guests alike. In the intimacy of Angela and Biagio's home that night, sitting across from one another, passing plates that had been in the family for generations, spilling cake crumbs on a crisply ironed heirloom tablecloth, drinking wine from the tiny cut crystal glasses that Biagio inherited from his grandfather, it was impossible not to feel welcomed, no matter what words were spoken.

CHAPTER NINE

We returned to California for the holidays and spent the winter there as we usually did, except that much of our thoughts and energy were far away, devoted to the ongoing reconstruction of our Italian home. Zef's work on the roof continued. There were dozens of phone calls made and photographs emailed back and forth from Mario, so we could keep abreast of progress. I was fascinated by all the dramatic changes in the house that I saw in the photos as the pixels emerged on my computer, but it certainly didn't feel like progress. The roof was fully gone at this point, and the rest of the structure looked eerily like an ancient ruin. I kept feeling like we were going backward rather than forward, but I suppose life is like that sometimes.

Zef continually reassured us in his calm way that all was going well. He explained to Kim and me that as soon as the cement collar was in place, he would be able to lay in the beautiful larch beams we had selected from the lumber mill to support our new roof, many of them 15" by 15" deep, and some over thirty feet long. The collar would also be 15" by 15", made more of steel reinforcement than cement, and fit all around the perimeter of the house. He would place it six inches away from the outside of the existing stone walls so that he could then lay stones to match the walls and seamlessly hide the collar. That is, and Zef always smiled when he said this, if the whole building didn't collapse from the weight of it.

Increasingly on those conference calls, the biggest topic of discussion became the foundation. Our house had none. All of those stones and bricks and all of that mud and cement had been sitting on dirt for hundreds of years. Now it was up to Zef, our geometras, and our structural engineer, to find a way to put a foundation beneath it all. Kim probed the team with a technical question: How do you undercut a three-hundred-year-old, two-foot-thick, twenty-foot-high stone wall to pour a foundation? Their answer was, you don't. They explained that, for our house, all we could really do is keep the walls from slipping sideways. So, around the perimeter of the entire building, they planned to excavate an area three feet wide and ten inches deep. Then, underneath the wall itself, every ten feet or so, they would clear another area just three feet long and ten inches deep where they would place steel rods poking out on either side, and pour concrete into the excavated area around the perimeter, forming a kind of sidewalk, *un marciapiede*. Finally, when they poured the interior floor, a ten-inch slab of concrete, it should all tie into the steel coming in under the walls from the sidewalk. Effectively, we would tie the entire bottom of the walls to the massive interior floor. Though Kim is not an engineer, he had built enough structures over the years to see the strength in this somewhat unique solution, which was all I needed to hear.

Technical, detailed discussions like this continued throughout the winter, with Kim sketching schematic designs for our geometras to finalize while he and I made decisions as best we could from a distance. But it became clear to both of us—at this precarious stage, we now both needed to come back to Italy armed with full suitcases and a plan to stay long enough to turn the deconstructing of our home into the rebuilding of it.

So, in early April, we flew again to Milan, rented a car for two full months, and made our way back to Roddino where Casa Piccola awaited us at Biagio and Angela's home.

We were now three years into the back-and-forth of this endeavor, and I noticed that each time we returned to Italy, it took a week or two to really ease into the relaxed ways of Piemonte and the little towns of Monforte and Roddino. Kim, especially, was forced to dial down from our fast-forward world in America to the one where we had nothing to do from twelve-thirty to three-thirty each day because all the stores were shuttered, and a nap actually became a sensible option. So, as usual, as the jet lag wore off, we slid into our daily drill. Go to the bank, stop, and have a coffee outside in the piazza. Go buy a newspaper, stop, and have a coffee in the piazza. Go to the bakery for breadsticks, stop, and have a coffee in the piazza. Then come home and take a nap.

My naps here have a life of their own. I do not take them. They take me. Like the mesmerizing scent of poppies in *The Wizard of Oz*, the warm afternoon breezes waft over me compelling me to lie down on the nearest bed and fall into a deep slumber. I awake an hour or so later, somewhat amazed at the profound satisfaction I feel. The first few times this happened, I stirred, wondering what time it was, when I heard the striking of a neighbor's cuckoo clock through the open window. Eyes still shut, I would count the cuckoos—one, two, three, four, five, six, seven . . . and so on. Had I been asleep for that many hours? Or was their clock so badly out of time? This happened a few times before I realized that it was not a clock at all. It was the real thing. A cuckoo bird, just flown in from over the mountains in Switzerland to wake me.

In Italy, I never worry too much about when I fall asleep or when I awake. In America, I wore a watch, set my alarm every morning, and the days were fully scheduled. Here, time just moves a little more slowly, morning and night. If we accomplished one solid task each day, I would be happy, even with our list. And the list was indeed long.

The new roof with old tiles that Zef finished did, in fact, stay firmly intact against the old walls. Our house had a structure, and we had begun work on the foundation. So next, we needed to find windows, doors, flooring, sinks, faucets, tiles, and so on. Of course, there is no Restoration Hardware, no Bed Bath & Beyond or even Lowe's Home Improvement anywhere near us. There is that place an hour away that sells flooring. And that other place fifty minutes away that sells flooring. There were maybe a dozen places that sell windows and doors, all a good hour away, and all with factories to be toured and advantages to be considered. The same with bathrooms and kitchens.

On many of the visits, especially for the more costly materials, Mario would accompany us and help translate the details in Italian to them, and in broken English to us. For me, the toughest part was setting the appointment, since it required me to make a telephone call, in Italian, with brand-new vocabulary such as *persiane*, *rubinetti*, and *piastrelle* and no ability to gesture or point to the shutters, faucets, and tiles to make myself understood. With a little prep and rehearsal time, and my Italian/English Dictionary in my lap, I could usually manage my phone calls, until they suggested an appointment for fifteen o'clock, and then I had a 50/50 chance of getting it right in Italian or English. My husband had more stamina for these endless and painstaking trips, but especially when Mario was not with us, I was doing much of the translating and found it draining trying to decipher the Italian words while simultaneously trying to understand the technical advantages of each of the different manufacturers. So we took these projects slowly.

Meanwhile, as our home was being constructed, so was our beautiful new way of life in the Langhe, and with each passing day we fell more in love with both.

Shopping for food in Italy was, for the most part, pure pleasure. For me, shopping in American supermarkets can be mildly agreeable and efficient, but often uninspiring. The proliferation of local farmers markets has changed all that, which is how the majority of Europeans have shopped for generations. When I was living in Paris, I awoke early and eagerly every Saturday morning just to arrive at the market at Avenue de Breteuil in time to see the most exotic fruits and vegetables, the widest ranges of cheeses, and the poultry, still with heads staring blankly, feet and skin attached, hanging in the stalls. When I lived in Frankfurt, the Kleinmarkthalle, a covered hall with lots of local vendors, set my pulse racing faster, as I discovered the vast selection of fresh herbs, mustards, new potatoes, root vegetables and meats, cheeses and sausages. In both of these cities, I loved the opportunity to interact with the local purveyors and to hone my primitive language skills. Once you have seen a wicker basket piled high with *des fraises* or *Erdbeeren* in early June, you remember the word for strawberry forever, in French and in German. In Monforte, I quickly learned they were *le fragole* and they were beauties.

Every Monday morning in Monforte there is the *mercato*, the outdoor market, rain or shine. It is fairly small, but it has three or four interesting fruit and vegetable stands, at which no single armful of produce ever seems to amount to more than a couple of euros. At the heart of the market is an admirably stocked cheese truck run by a gregarious family that willingly works with my husband as he practices his Italian on them: "*Due etti Parmesan stagionata, et un mezzo chilo di prosciutto cotto, per favore.*" We also discovered that our Roddino neighbors, Roberto and Carla, just up the hill from us, make bread for most of the finer restaurants in the area. They keep a bread stand at the market, which we always visit, although even better is when we walk over to their home and watch them baking their fragrant loaves. On the lower level of their home, they have a full-on bakery with an oven, which is twelve feet deep and can bake one hundred loaves at once. It is remarkable. Whenever we stop by, we stock up on their famous bread, sometimes still warm, and always add on some of their breadsticks roasted in olive oil. In Monforte's market there is a fish stand where no one ever buys anything because it is Monday and everyone knows the fishermen don't fish on Sunday. And then there is the guy who sells spit-roasted chickens and short fat French fries whose provocative aromas make you salivate and the idea of eating a bag of hot fries at ten in the morning suddenly sound sensible. Everything is just picked fresh and in season, and apart from the bananas and an occasional pineapple, it is all grown or raised nearby.

The etiquette is to never touch the produce. That would be rude to the customers that follow. Instead, you point, tell the seller how much you would like, and he or she picks the best ones for you and places them in a little brown sack. By contrast, in a large Italian supermarket, the produce rules are quite different. You put on plastic gloves to protect the food, gently select your own fruit and vegetables, weigh them, put them in a paper bag, then place the ticket with the weight and price on the bag before putting them in your cart. If you forget to do this, I happen to know, you arrive at checkout, the checkout person raises her eyebrows at you, and everyone in line behind you frowns at you while she clicks her heels walking all the way back to the fruit and vegetable section of the store to weigh and mark the fruit for you. This is not a pleasant moment in your day, nor in the day of the people behind you. Fortunately, in the outdoor markets, there is no danger of this happening.

There is a far larger market on Tuesdays and Saturdays in the town next to ours, Dogliani. The Dogliani market runs for blocks and blocks through the old town, spilling into the two piazzas on either side. The same fruit and vegetable people are there, and the same cheese family and the other merchants are there, but there is also the olive man, two or three good fish stands, the fresh pasta cart, and maybe a hundred other purveyors to visit. On Wednesdays and Saturdays there is a grand market in Alba, half an hour away, that is even bigger than the one in Dogliani, but all have the same seasonal farm fresh products, year in, year out.

When I washed the vegetables and fruit, I noticed that they often still had clumps of soil clinging to them, almost as an assurance of freshness. Our perfectly cleaned and comparatively sterile produce in America must feel suspicious to these folks who nearly all have abundant home gardens and orchards. I always need to rinse and scrub the celery and carrots and potatoes two or three times longer here. It is a small price to pay for such an authentically fresh taste. In all of the markets, outdoor, local, and even the supermarkets, the flavors are rich and true. Even with packaged goods or frozen, branded products, if the food is not absolutely delicious, it doesn't sell. Italians won't stand for mediocrity, be it in a canned soup or a frozen entrée, or what we now call artisanal foods. It is simply how they eat. All the time.

Meat in the Langhe is another world entirely. Veal is king. Not the tortured, colorless, flavorless veal that all my friends in America have sworn off. What is done to those poor animals to keep the flesh pale and tender is a crime, and I stay away from it in America, too. But here, huge, white cattle roam the hillsides munching on the sweet grasses. They are a particular breed of animal called Bovine Langhe. They are strange-looking creatures, gnarly, brawny, and lean. They have no visible fat on them, but their muscle fibers are short and crisscrossed in a way that keeps the meat from being at all tough. It is as lean as chicken and as tender as well-marbled beef. The animals live a happy but short life on well-tended farms and are slaughtered just before they turn two years old, so they can still be considered veal. These farms fuel the local economy and keep the countryside green. It is a wonderful way to support farmers, and to eat healthy protein. You also find pork, in salamis, sausages, prosciuttos, chops, and roasts. But veal is what Piemonte does better than anyone, and it is part of what makes the food here so uniquely good. I beg my friends, when they come, to open their minds to this kind of veal when in Piemonte, and nearly all but the strictest vegetarians become converts. I have.

My favorite butcher shop, or *macelleria*, is small and sparkling clean and white, one of the few places in the area that is cool and air-conditioned. There is always a line of people waiting to be served by the three or four butchers running back and forth, grabbing a hunk of meat from the case, masterfully slicing and pounding it precisely to order, offering a smile and a suggestion for cooking, occasionally sharing a bit of town gossip if they can catch their breath long enough. To the right of the countertop is a large sign detailing the animal's name, the date that the particular cow was born, the date it was slaughtered, and where and by whom it was raised, usually within a mile or two of the shop. Inspecting the case, you can see that, indeed, there are the various parts that make up just that one animal. Legs. Steaks. The bony ribs. The purply liver. The tail, sliced crosswise in little disks for oxtail soup. And the two kinds of minced beef, one for meatballs and sausages, and one very lean and red, ready to be eaten raw, as *carne cruda*.

When all that meat is gone, they wipe down the case, sterilize it, and then bring in the next animal. I love to bring home a *tagliata*, a little steak, for Kim and me to grill. He sears it quickly, keeping it fairly rare, and slices it on the diagonal like a mini London broil. In an old local cookbook, I discovered a Piemontese sauce for it, *bagnetto verde*, or green bath. It uses two fistfuls of parsley and some mint leaves, chopped finely, salt capers (a food group all their own), fresh lemon juice with its zest, toasted bread crumbs, red pepper flakes, and some life-changingly lusty anchovies all smashed together into a thick paste. With a few hefty glugs of good olive oil to thin it, and some chunky sea salt, it is ready to serve alongside the steak, or on anything else you like to eat for the next several days. Even people who hate anchovies love this sauce. You never need to tell anyone they are in there, and everyone will wonder at that deliciously addictive flavor.

But the cheese is my real weakness. Toma is the name of the local cheese you will find in any of the markets and cheese shops throughout the region, but it is just as often referred to as Tuma, which is Piemontese dialect, and it comes in dozens of different varieties like Tomini, Robbiola, or my favorite, Langherino. Their names can be paired with the town of their origin, like Tuma di Bossolasco, just a few miles from our home, or Tuma di Anna, made in the cheese mecca of Murazzano, a little Alpen hamlet on the way to Monviso. Some Tumas taste as fresh as butter and as soft as cream cheese, soft enough that I cut it with a spoon, and are meant to be eaten in a few days, maybe draped with anchovies and a delicious basily green sauce. Or they can be aged for as long as three months, wonderful for melting over bread or for serving alongside fruit. The shape of this cheese is almost always round and thick, like a Camembert, or sometimes taller. It can be made from either cow, sheep, or goat's milk, or often in some combination of the three. All of the milk that comes from the animals here yields incredibly creamy, tangy cheese, as well as butter and cream, and the milk from the cows in the highest Alps is particularly prized. One night at the restaurant Guido, I tasted plain vanilla ice cream made by their chef from cows that roam the mountain meadows at eight-thousand feet, and believe me, it was startlingly more delicious than any ice cream I had ever eaten before. No wonder the cheeses made from those Alpine milks are what Italians enjoy for dessert.

The noble hazelnut, which in America is the most underrated of nuts, makes its presence known in so many of the dishes here, both innovative and traditional. It is the essential flavor of Italian chocolate, unlike the peanut profile used in Mars and Hershey's chocolates, and it makes for less cloyingly sweet confections. The Piemontese also use hazelnuts the way we use almonds and pistachios, in salads, desserts, and in savory sauces that might top pasta or meat. Or they can be featured in sweet sauces that include honey, mustard, or wine and are draped over meats for holidays. It took me about a day to get used to the different nuances of hazelnuts, and now it is a taste I associate with everything I love about Italy.

It is, I believe, no coincidence that just a few towns over, twenty minutes away, is the town of Bra. It is where the hospital and the immigration office can be found, and it is where the concept of Slow Food, a counterrevolution to fast food, was born. Carlo Petrini started the movement, first enlisting the help of the pope, then the Catholic Church and the Italian government. Upon hearing of plans for a McDonald's on the Spanish Steps in Rome in 1986, Petrini went to the Catholic Church and the government asking them to intercede. In 1989, his Slow Food movement became the first organized plan to preserve, respect, and reinforce local farms and farmers, small food growers, and producers. It promotes the traditions of local, seasonal food, which is not only the most delicious but also the healthiest way to eat, along with the culture that fosters this way of life, one that has been sustained for generations. Petrini won their support to maintain Italian food culture as it is and this is now encouraged by the Church and the Italian government. The Slow Food idea has been celebrated in America thanks to Alice Waters and other respected chefs and food writers who have embraced and championed the idea. It is impossible to argue with. Taking the time to grow the best food, cultivate, cook, and enjoy it, is just one of the things that makes life here such a pleasure, every day, at every meal. It is how it has always been in Piemonte, and now, hopefully, how it always will be.

Spending time in Italy was teaching me, firsthand, how something as primal as eating, and as simple as shopping, as essential as being part of a small community, creates a life. Living like this, more slowly, more purposefully, and more enjoyably, changes who I am. It means I, too, slow down and truly listen to the sounds around me, better savor tastes and smells. When I am here, I am more aware of the people around me and laugh a little more fully, love a little more unguardedly. I enjoy what I eat, what I drink, and how I feel because of it.

I realize that each moment in the Langhe is truly a treasure. And so many small, incremental moments in the day add up to this joyful new life.

Photos Under construction

****Bagnetto Verde****

4–5 of the best quality anchovies you can find, preferably from
   a jar
2 cups fresh Italian flat-leafed parsley
1 cup fresh mint leaves
2 tablespoons capers packed in salt, rinsed very well
1 medium lemon
¼ teaspoon red pepper flakes
1 cup or more of excellent virgin olive oil
⅓ cup bread crumbs (not panko), toasted to a golden brown
Flaky sea salt and freshly cracked pepper, as needed, to taste

Rinse and dry the anchovies. Set aside. On a large cutting board, mince the parsley and mint together. Add the anchovies and capers, and chop all together quite finely. Then use the side of the knife to mash the ingredients together and form a rough paste. Place the mixture in a glass bowl. Using a microplane or grater, grate the zest of the lemon over the herb mixture. Squeeze the juice from the naked lemon, strain out the seeds, and add the juice to the mixture as well. Add in the pepper flakes. Now add the oil, little by little, beating with a wooden spoon until the sauce is well blended but still quite loose, reserving some of the oil to use at the end if needed. Add the bread crumbs, little by little, to thicken. You may not need to use the full amount. Let the mixture set for at least an hour, then adjust salt and pepper to taste. It should still be fairly loose and sauce-like. Add more oil if needed. Serve with grilled meats, or over cheese or grilled vegetables. If refrigerated, the sauce will be just as delicious the next day.

CHAPTER TEN

One day, with the spring melting snows on the Alps, Alpen rivers rushing full force and wildflowers in bloom, Angela and Biagio invited us on a trip to the mountains. Happy to take a break from the day-to-day decisions and questions that come with construction, we accepted, gladly, *volentieri*. Although the ski slopes and resorts were boarded up for the season, they were confident we would find a trattoria or osteria somewhere along the way for lunch. So off we set, the four of us in one car.

The Langhe is named for its hilltop ridges, and we meandered along those ridges, looking down on either side of the road at the patchwork of vineyards and hazelnut orchards on either side, paths carved like jigsaws between the rows for tractors and workers. The vines were just starting out again, as they do every spring, optimistic little sprouts drinking in the warm sun and light rains. The hazelnut trees were budding green, neat and orderly. Life was good.

We drove through the Po River Valley, alongside apple orchards, cornfields, and farms. No wonder Napoleon loved this area, I thought to myself. It fed his troops so effortlessly, and the Piemontese soldiers, with their sturdy constitutions and unmatched work ethic, made him a victor and a hero.

Soon we were winding up through the Alps, past little stone villages and fields of flowers that Heidi must have run through. An hour or so later, we arrived at the base of Prato Nevoso, or Snowy Meadow. I was absolutely ready to climb out of the car after all that touring around those curves and take in some fresh air and spectacular scenery. Right in front of me stretched a gigantic and thoroughly empty parking lot that, in season, probably sports thousands of cars. But behind it stood a towering range of princely mountains that, even on that dry spring day, set my heart racing. The view was inspiring as we strolled about and made me wish I still skied.

The shuttered ski village was a ghost town. But we poked around the various streets and finally found one trattoria with its doors open, so we entered and seated ourselves. A gentleman came over to take our order and Angela, without glancing at the menu, ordered polenta. I can't remember what the rest of us ordered, but in the end we all wanted to eat Angela's lunch.

As much as I go on and on about how amazing the food is here, I need to confess that, for the most part, the bread is not amazing. Our neighbor Roberto's bread is the decided exception, which may be why it is being adopted by so many of the better restaurants. And, of course, focaccia is nearly always a tender, crunchy delight to behold. But the everyday bread in most stores and restaurants is, to my American-grown palette, a little insipid. I missed the tangy, crusty San Francisco sourdough I had grown up with. Traditionally, Italians make their bread soft, with little or no salt, and any baker knows that salt is what gives bread flavor. Perhaps a bread, light on flavor with a soft texture, functions better as a tool to sop up delicious sauces; I don't know. I do know that this tiny trattoria, in which, by the way, we are the only guests, had killer bread. We smelled it while we were ordering, and they brought it out minutes later, hot, crusted, flavorful, and perfect. I ate five pieces. With butter.

Summoning all of my Italian and any drop of charm I may have inherited from my mother, I complimented the chef who, as it turned out, is also the owner, the maître d', and the waiter, and asked him if we could possibly buy a loaf or two of his *buonissimo* bread to bring home. He said he was sorry, but no, this last basket was all there was of it. Disappointed, but undaunted, I promised that we would come back another time and hoped that maybe he would have some extra then.

It was a delightful lunch and even though the four of us had only about a hundred words in common, we all enjoyed a lively and entertaining conversation. It is hard to describe how we manage to communicate, but it is often something like this:

INTERIOR RESTAURANT, AT TABLE

ANGELA (ORDERING): *Polenta, per favore.*

KIM (TO ANGELA): *Polenta?? É buona??*

ANGELA: *Sì, sì! Molto buona!*

BARBARA: *Non conosco polenta.* (I am not familiar with polenta.)

KIM (TO BARBARA): It's like grits.

BARBARA (TO ALL): Oh, well, I don't like grits. *Non mi piacciono grits.*

BIAGIO: *Cosa sono?? Grits???* (What? What are grits??)

BARBARA: *Sì. Come polenta, ma sono della Louisiana.* (Like polenta, but they are from Louisiana.)

BIAGIO: *Non conosco Louisiana.* (I am not familiar with Louisiana.)

BARBARA: *Mia mamma era della Louisiana, e a mio papa piacciono molto grits!!!* (My mom was from Louisiana and my father adored grits!)

BIAGIO: (smiling) *Capito!!* (I understand!)

THE POLENTA ARRIVES, AND ANGELA SHARES A SMALL PORTION WITH KIM AND BARBARA. BARBARA TASTES IT, SWOONS AT ITS DELICIOUSNESS.

BARBARA: Ahhhh. *Capito tutto!!!* (Now I understand.) *E buonissimo!!!*

Angela smiles, pleased. Kim orders another bowl for himself to go with his lasagna.

Our conversation went on more or less like that for the rest of the delicious lunch. We paid the bill and as we were in the car pulling out of our parking space, the owner/chef/waiter came running out after us carrying a bundle swaddled in napkins. It was a loaf of bread, still warm and fragrant from the oven. He had made another loaf just for us while we ate. When I tried to pay him, he refused. "*Un regalino*," he said. A small gift.

After that intoxicating first taste of the Alps, I longed to return and, next time, explore the mountain that graces the distant skyline from our backyard, the one that stands tauntingly thousands of feet higher than all the others around it, the twelve-thousand-foot-high Monviso. So, a few weeks later, one steamy day in late May, Kim and I left Zef and his workers working away in Roddino and headed due west, in search of the still snow-covered mountain peak. The journey began with a straight, flat drive across the valley for about an hour. Then a curving ascent of six thousand feet over the next twenty minutes brought us to a world of storybook houses with old slate roofs situated in grassy meadows filled with wandering cows wearing bells around their necks. Cool mountain air, a rushing river, and refreshing breezes change the temperature, and your mood. This is Crissolo, where true hikers, trekkers, and rock climbers congregate to finish the last six thousand feet of vertical on foot. It is also where we climbed out of the car to eat.

There are a few pizzerias, ice cream shops, and trattorias that serve the various tourists, but the very last one you come to, a small restaurant across from the river, is packed with locals, workers and families alike. As soon as we sat down, I realized why Angela chose polenta at our last lunch in the Alps. Rustic and hearty, polenta seems to be the star attraction on all the menus in these little mountain towns. Never before had polenta been part of my consideration set, but remembering Angela's, I ordered it. The osteria owner appeared shortly, carrying an oval platter smothered with the golden mush, smooth, creamy, and buttery, then set out an assortment of toppings on the table alongside. Soft and velvety gorgonzola, tangy herbed sour cream, a sweet raspberry sauce, and a rich, meaty ragu were offered, and with each different topping, the polenta tasted entirely different and entirely delicious. Then I understood. Polenta is pleasing to Italians in the same way we might enjoy a big taco dinner: fun, celebratory, yet simple, and with a variety of toppings to satisfy everyone's taste. My husband ordered the *Pasta alla Carbonara*, made *in casa* with locally made raschera cheese and crispy pancetta, so meltingly good, the memory of it spoiled him for any other *Pasta alla Carbonara* he has ordered since.

Amply fortified, we, like the tinkling cows dotting the mountainside, headed out to stroll through the cool meadows with Monviso's snowy peak towering over our shoulders. Countless tiny wildflowers were scattered here and there, and a humble little stream sprang from a pile of rocks at the far end of the field. Next to it was a hand-painted sign announcing that this little trickle, shallow and narrow enough to straddle, was the headwaters to the mighty Po River, Italy's longest and most vital waterway. I wondered what adventures these little drops of water, splashing about, had ahead of them as they ventured south and east to the Adriatic Sea. Standing there, looking back through the peaks and down along the valley, I could almost make out the hills where our new/old home was under reconstruction, and I only fleetingly contemplated what might lie ahead for us.

We climbed back in the car and carefully made our way down the precarious gravelly trail that serves as a road, until we were just past Crissolo. Suddenly there were three cars ahead of us, stopped dead in the road. What kind of a traffic jam could there be up here? I heard men shouting in Piemontese, and we inched our way forward until we were completely surrounded by dozens and dozens of cows rumbling down the road, prodded by these men. We rolled down the windows and on either side we were eye to eye with their fuzzy faces for a good ten minutes, until finally we were able to ease by, or actually through, them. We continued on with all the windows down and their unmistakable aroma wasn't completely blown out of the car until just before we arrived home to Casa Piccola.

Three days later, I was once again sitting in a darkened airline cabin watching the screen on the seat back in front of me as the blue icon of my plane crept imperceptibly across the Atlantic like a kite with an endless tail, toward San Francisco International Airport. We were going home. We were going back to our Starbucks, the *Today Show*, and to the soft gray fog rolling in every evening. Soon, we would be back at our gym across the street and the crab place on the Embarcadero, an easy drive away from Kim's parents' rest home and a perfectly clear phone call away from any of our friends, most in our same time zone. It was perfect. The life we had retired to was perfect. I loved San Francisco, had spent an idyllic childhood in the Bay Area and the first ten years of my advertising career in the city itself. It was my home.

So why did I feel so torn? After decades of an adrenaline-rich career, pummeling around the world and waiting for happiness to find me, it had. I was in love with my husband and the life we were living. It felt somehow like the movie had ended happily, but too soon. I was not quite ready to say, "This is it. This is my life now back in the town where I grew up, happily ever after. Familiar, easy and comfortable." Where was the challenge in that? Where was the thrill of discovering the word for birds (*uccelli*) or the first boozy taste of a sugared sweet and tender breakfast panettone on Easter morning? When I was in San Francisco, I missed the evenings of looking out our window and wondering if Napoleon and his soldiers really had scrambled up the hill across the valley like they said he had, or dashing into town after dinner in the lingering twilight for a short promenade and a tangerine gelato. And I surely missed the extraordinary earthly pleasures of daily coffee in the piazza or slipping into the Barolo Bar for a glass of Nebbiolo, a plate of prosciutto, and a hug from Silvia as a new guitarist played American rock and roll sung with an Italian accent.

It was always in my heart.

❊❊❊*Creamy Polenta with Gorgonzola*❊❊❊

4 cups water, salted
1 scant cup of polenta flour, either instant or coarsely ground
  regular polenta
1 cup of gorgonzola cheese, cubed
½ cup grated Parmesan cheese
Additional salt and pepper to taste
Olive oil

In a medium saucepan bring the salted water to a boil. Lower the heat to moderate and add the polenta in a slow, steady stream, whisking constantly until polenta and water are fully incorporated. Continue whisking to be sure there are no lumps. Instant polenta will take about 10 minutes to achieve this; regular polenta will take 30 to 40 minutes. Add ¾ of the gorgonzola cubes until melted and reduce to a simmer, uncovered, stirring occasionally until the polenta is smooth, thick, and creamy. Add the remaining ¼ cup of gorgonzola and the Parmesan cheese and stir for a minute, then cover and turn off the heat. Let it rest for 5 minutes. The result should be a smooth, creamy polenta with little bits of melted cheese chunks on top. Ladle into individual bowls, drizzle with a little olive oil, salt and pepper, and, if desired, pass the Parmesan. Serve hot.

CHAPTER ELEVEN

Of course, once we settled back into our home in San Francisco I appreciated the many joys that presented themselves there, with my new marriage and my new family. From the day I met Kim, I was intrigued, although it took weeks, even months, before I knew it was love. But he came with three young sons as part of the package, and with them it was love at first sight. The handsome young teenager and nine-year-old twins melted my heart immediately. I have never liked the word stepson, because it sounds like a stutter, a hesitation, like something less than. Forgive me if I refer to them as our sons, because that is how they feel to me.

And that June, our son Flynn and his girlfriend, Katherine, along with their enthusiastic fifty-pound dog, came to spend a week with us in our little apartment, leaving me with a sore belly from laughing so much. Next, Flynn's twin, Kelly, came out to interview for graduate school in San Francisco, and again, my muscles ached from laughing by the time his visit was done. Our oldest son, Cooper, and his new bride, Allie, came to visit for a few nights, too, on a trip from their home in Asia. Living so far away, their visits were rare and exciting and I always savored every moment with them, listening to their insights and astute take on the changing world around us. And, of course, there is constantly plenty of laughter to go around with them as well.

Besides family, we enjoyed time with our neighbors. Our little community at 101 Lombard Street had Wednesday night barbecues by the pool, and since it was summer in San Francisco, we all bundled up in warm coats around the grill eating and shivering, while comparing recipes for the appetizers and desserts we each brought to the party. Concerts were regularly held on the pier across the street, and we could hear the strains of music floating in from across our balcony on the breezy summer evenings. I felt happy.

Still, I often found myself thinking and wondering about how things were going with the house in Italy. Like a lover in a long-distance relationship, I was living my life on the outside, but inside, my heart was always full of elsewhere. Was Zef on schedule? Did the paint colors work with the stones and bricks? What would we ever do to landscape that huge muddy mess of a yard? Kim and I talked every night at dinner in detail about all these things, wondering when we should return to finally finish our home in Italy.

It did not take long. By August, we decided we must go back again. The entire kitchen was still to be measured and appliances and cabinets needed to be ordered. It was time to finalize and install our floors and windows, and we needed to select our sinks, fixtures, and tile, which, for me, would be the really fun part. So, once more, my suitcase, barely put away from the last trip, was packed and ready for autumn in the Langhe, as was I. The wine country as harvest approaches is the most exciting time of year, with raucous autumn color in every square inch of vineyards, and orchards and forests aflame in the lingering afternoon light. I had learned that. And my heart was full in anticipation of it again now.

We arrived at Casa Piccolo in Roddino in the late afternoon, and before unpacking, before even getting the key from Biagio, we raced across the yard to see the progress Zef and his team had made. The foundation was in, which gave an aura of permanence to the former-barn/soon-to-be-home. Roof on, walls up, cement floor poured. But unlike in a finished home, there was a giant tractor in the downstairs bedroom. And the only way to reach the upstairs was with Zef's twelve-foot ladder, which meant I would not be going upstairs anytime soon. But just being in the structure again was thrilling beyond words.

The next day, reality took over. Having signed one contract with Zef for the roof, and then another for the foundation, we now needed to sign additional ones for finishing the house. There would be separate contracts for the plumbing, electrical work, doors and windows, floors and tiles, as well as for the landscaping and pool. Mario had helped guide us in the selection of many of the subcontractors, but each contract required that we sign and date every page, amounting to hundreds of pages and signatures. The fingers on my right hand hurt before we were finished. I had never seen so much paperwork for anything I had ever been a part of in my life, and even Kim, who spent his entire thirty-year career creating and developing real estate, said the same thing. The thoroughness of the documents was impressive. Maddeningly laborious, but impressive. We sat one long afternoon in the geometra's office signing page after page, and the formality and finality of it felt wonderful, in spite of my sore hand. I was learning that as relaxed and informal as Italy could be, doing business there could be quite bureaucratic.

Then, after leaving the signing, we went with Mario to our bank to deposit the money for the contracts. Mario pulled Kim aside, and I walked ahead to the car to wait.

When Kim returned, he said, "That was strange."

"What?"

"Mario asked me for another fee, in addition to the overall construction fee we have been paying him. He said it was customary. I have never heard of such a thing. He insisted on cash, a lot of it—three thousand euros."

"Really?"

"He promised me he would get me a receipt. But I told him, next time we would need to know about this in advance." We drove home, both feeling unsettled about the transaction.

Kim, who is the most thorough record keeper I have ever known, spent the next few days going through his files, analyzing all of the contracts, subcontracts, and purchases that had taken place with Mario's involvement. He was starting to see that in addition to the occasional, cash-only fees Mario had randomly been asking for, it was likely that Mario had been getting kick-backs from many of the suppliers he had introduced us to, money that he had never disclosed to us. Kim could not be sure in each case exactly how much Mario was receiving, but with all that we had spent on the finishes, it added up to a substantial amount. And that was in addition to a fee of three percent that we had agreed to pay him on our construction costs. We went back to our bank and showed them our paperwork, and they agreed that what Mario had done was unethical and most likely illegal. We had been scammed, and he had also taken advantage of our suppliers. Kim and I decided we needed to confront Mario and let him know that he needed to be completely transparent with us or we could not work with him anymore. We invited him over to talk with us that evening, and Mario agreed to come.

But before Kim could tell him about the irregularities that he had uncovered, Mario began to hang his head, and nearly cried, saying that his wife was out in the car, and had told him to "be a man" and ask us for money. He said if Kim and I would give him money, we could become investors in Mario's new company, though it was unclear what exactly that company was. He promised us a high percentage return. Only ten thousand dollars would be needed, and he needed it now. In cash.

Kim, of course, said no. He also said he was aware of the money that had been exchanging hands that we had not heard about. Mario denied any wrongdoing, but looked very uncomfortable.

Kim said, "You may be able to convince yourself that skimming money or taking fees on our behalf that we are not aware of is okay. But it is not. We are sorry this happened, but our relationship is over."

Mario left, embarrassed and awkward, and I felt like I had lost a friend. We did not know him the way we thought we had, and felt betrayed. It hurt. In all of our time in Italy, he was the solitary person who had treated us with such disregard and dishonesty, and we realized that we would be better off without him. We spoke with all of the people he had introduced us to, and let them know we would not be including Mario in any of our business dealings going forward. They all agreed, and did not seem surprised, saying that they absolutely understood our position. And that was the end of that story.

The whole experience left me feeling both sad and foolish. But dishonest people are everywhere, and when I think of the scores of good people and friends we had met, it more than makes up for this one opportunistic scoundrel.

That August in Piemonte was warmer and wetter than usual, occasionally with magnificent thunder and hailstorms. The grapes, green and firm, were growing bigger and hanging like udders along the vines. Zef's men came and went, never complaining about the heat, working every day but Sunday from eight in the morning until sundown. They were creating the thirty-eight stone stairs that reach from the parking area up above the house down to the front door. One muggy day, after a violent thunder and lightning display, there was a torrential hailstorm that caused a giant cascading waterfall from the top of the stairs all the way to our front door, which came within inches of flooding our home. The workers stood in our doorway with us, watching the power of nature and we all thrilled at the energy in the air. Then, as suddenly as it arrived, the storm passed. Barely missing a beat, the men dug out the mud pushing against our front door and went back to work. That same August, however, resulted in a rough year for many of the winemakers because of the wild weather, and that one hailstorm alone completely took out several acres of grapes in the next town over. A year's worth of work gone, in a matter of minutes. Advertising is not exactly known for being a secure and nurturing career choice, but I cannot imagine the life of a winemaker, or any farmer, so dependent on the capriciousness of the weather. It is humbling.

September arrived, and with it, our first guests, that is, aside from Rob and Carolyn who I have always thought of more as co-conspirators than guests. Cooper and Allie had come all the way from their home in Asia to Monforte, open and curious as ever to see our new adventure. Since Casa Piccola was barely big enough for the two of us, they agreed to spend a few nights at Grappolo D'Oro, the albergo in Monforte's main piazza, and a few nights out in the countryside at an agriturismo within walking distance of our place.

Allie arrived alone, a few days ahead of Cooper, who had business in Germany. She is very smart and clever, with young, excellent taste, and I loved that she embraced our project so wholeheartedly, climbing around the construction site with us, joining us on door and window factory tours, asking questions and offering suggestions. It was she who found stacks and stacks of old hand-painted Piemontese tiles under a pile of rubbish behind one of our outbuildings. Together, we spent days scrubbing the tiles with wire brushes in Biagio's icy well water, revealing their amazingly soft, faded beauty of golds, pinks, and grays. Ultimately, they would comprise the prettiest floor in the house, as they were exactly enough for the floor in the guest bath. We took Allie to the Slow Food Cheese Festival in nearby Bra, where she and Kim wandered for hours among the stalls, finding new cheeses and some favorite American ones, which we procured and enjoyed for the rest of their visit. And then, on my birthday, Allie presented me with an armload of wildflowers she had gathered for me on a walk, placing them in a vase on the plastic table on the terrace of Casa Piccola. I took a photo of the flowers, and it remains one of my favorite gifts, ever.

Cooper arrived a few days later. Even taller than his father, perceptive and wise beyond his years, he joined us on our daily outings, thoughtfully taking everything in. I noticed that he seemed to reserve judgment for a while, focusing his energies on inspecting the property, asking many intelligent questions, and then enjoying several days with us touring the hill towns, wine tasting at Monforte's magnificent Conterno Fantino, and lingering over a long truffle-laden lunch al fresco at the restaurant Bovio in the nearby town of La Morra.

My husband and I were like little kids, excited to show them everything we had discovered and loved about the Langhe, Monforte, and Roddino, hoping that they would share that love. But I was a little nervous. I could certainly imagine that the area may not be to everyone's taste. There are no famous monuments, no busy shopping areas, no well-curated museums, to be sure. In the dozen or so years that I had known them, Cooper and Allie had grown into fairly cosmopolitan adults; this rural life might not appeal to them. But I also knew that Cooper, like his father, was not afraid of a road less traveled. Both he and Allie made the decision to walk away from secure jobs in New York, and to live and work abroad in Asia for the experience and adventure of it. And like his father, Cooper (as well as Allie) was open to exploring all that the big world had to offer, before starting a family. So I thought they, of all people, might understand what we were doing. Finally, over dinner on the night before they were about to leave, Kim asked his son point blank what he thought of our project, and our new home. I had not realized until that moment how much their endorsement was part of the dream. It wasn't just a vacation place; it was a home for all of us, for Kim and me, and for his three boys and the families they would create. Cooper's words have become engraved in our hearts:

"I get it. Absolutely. The Langhe is authentic. It is everything that is wonderful about Italy, but without tourists."

Sage and salient as always, he succinctly captured the spirit that we had fallen in love with here. It is real. And it is beautiful. At least, it is to me.

Shortly after Cooper and Allie left, we began packing up to return again to San Francisco for the fall and winter. We toured the house one last time, walking through and discussing the various details with Zef. That is when Zef first told us he believed we would be able to actually take occupancy of the house when we came back in March. Occupancy. It was a tantalizing concept. Throughout those past few months, we had made good progress. We had a roof, walls, windows, doors, some plumbing and heating. We had plans for our flooring and lighting and were beginning to talk about how we might landscape. Of course, we had no stairs to take us to our bedroom, nor toilets, sinks, or countertops. Ever the optimist, Zef may have been overstating the timing. But we, too, could begin to see our house taking shape. Our home in Italy, our dream, was becoming real.

Then it occurred to me, something I had felt quietly growing from deep in my heart for some time. I needed still more of Italy. I needed more of this house, soon to be a home. We had always thought it would become just our second home, a place to escape to in summers with friends and a place where all of our children and their future families could be together. That certainly could never be the case with our two-bedroom apartment in San Francisco. That is why, from day one, Kim and I designed this house with an eye to his three sons and their partners (now, my family) feeling like this was their home, too.

But more and more I was feeling that I no longer wanted to go back and forth and divide my time and my energy between two homes. I wanted to really know this country. I wanted to feel the rhythm of the year, its seasons, its holidays, its soul. I wanted to come back and stay in the Langhe for an entire year. Maybe more.

So that winter, we began to think differently. I refocused my energy and began to search for options, for possibilities. It was time to get serious, to get creative, and to find a way to make this dream a reality.

Like most people, we do not and never will have endless resources. So, if we wanted to live abroad for a full year, we would either have to work there, or find another way to get by. Actually buying the old stone house had been the least of it. It was in such disrepair when we found it, like so many abandoned homes in the area, it was not terribly expensive. But the work we were doing recently required us to reach into our savings at every turn, for every sink, every light fixture, literally every stick and stone. We were as careful as we could be about getting multiple bids for everything, especially now that Mario was gone. But at some point, we realized, we had to either stop building or commit fully. And my heart already was fully committed, as was Kim's.

We talked about how Kim could continue to work remotely from Italy for the year, and return to the States occasionally to look in on his remaining projects when needed. I had a few clients I continued to work for, and I could do that from Italy as well. But we would still need to sublet our apartment in San Francisco to cover our mortgage there. It took a gut-wrenching moment of fortitude to face that reality, but it was necessary. Going through a local rental agent, we found a couple who wanted a one-year rental agreement to move into our San Francisco home in the spring. I was comforted knowing that if this new adventure abroad turned out badly, we could come back to San Francisco, pick up the pieces, and get back to our lives there.

We also decided to ship our car to Italy. Renting a car in Italy was prohibitively expensive, and in order to buy a car there, we needed Italian residency, a months-long proposition, at best. Our car was seven years old, still ran well, and was far more comfortable than most European cars for someone as tall as my husband, so it all made sense. The day the moving truck came for the car was when the enormity of what we were doing all suddenly felt real. We watched from the sidewalk as they set up a ramp from the street to the truck, drove the car into the container, and banged the door shut with loud finality. It was like waving goodbye to a friend heading out on a transatlantic crossing. I fleetingly wondered if I would actually ever see the car again. But, no, that couldn't possibly happen, could it?

Throughout that winter, I spent time mentally sorting what we could take with us. It was surprisingly satisfying paring down, eliminating the clutter, and selecting only the few things I would not want to live without: a cloisonne bowl of my mother's, her cast iron frying pan, an old chair that had belonged to my father and grandfather. Those went into a small crate. The rest was donated, thrown away, or put in storage. Life felt suddenly lighter.

We then organized our day-to-day life, our bills, taxes, and such mundane details, so that it could be handled virtually. Working with the Italian Consulate General in San Francisco, we began the process of trying to qualify as residents of Italy, in order to make living there that much easier. There would be far more to do to finish the process, once we arrived in Italy. Americans do not need visas to travel to Europe, of course, but if we wanted to be able to stay for months on end, it would be better to have our *permesso di soggiorno*. And if we ever decide to buy another car, or if we want to go to school there, we would need to be residents as well. Our *permesso di soggiorno* also gives us the ability to qualify for health care. Fortunately, although we are partially retired, we are both very healthy, so we felt this was all just in case.

We began saying goodbye to our friends. It tugged on my heart each time. I told them I would see them soon, in just a year, and that the time would fly by, as it always does. Our neighbors Rusty and Paula threw a party for us in their apartment, with a dozen or so other friends. My friend Judy had bought me a beautiful linen grocery sack, hand painted with a watercolor of the San Francisco Farmers Market. She was thrilled with it, because she knew I would think of my friends every week when I took it to our farmers market in Monforte, and she was right. That night, some of our friends, like Linda and Jim, and Marcy and David, promised they would come visit as soon as we were settled. It made those goodbyes easier.

Saying goodbye to family was harder. My parents, of course, were both watching me from heaven, so I would feel as close to them in Italy as anywhere else on Earth. A couple of long phone calls and long hugs comprised the goodbyes to my two brothers. They were happy for me, so we all took it in stride. Perhaps they were getting used to their little sister's vagabond ways, moving here and there over the decades. Kim's three siblings were already planning when they would visit us, too, so that eased the sting with them.

The most difficult farewell was to Kim's mother. Even when living an hour away, every time we kissed her goodbye, we were aware that the future was uncertain. At ninety-three, she was as sharp as ever and remarkably healthy, living in a seniors community with the most wonderful care. And although Kim's father had passed away a few years earlier, she seemed to be happy, with lots of friends, her church, and her caregivers to see to her daily needs. We went to stay with her at her community's guest room for several days before getting on our plane. We were able to have all our meals together, and had time for leisurely chats about big and small things. But finally, the time came for us to head to the airport. Ever the lady, she kissed us goodbye, tenderly, with a smile on her face. We promised her we would return for a visit before the year was out, and we reminded ourselves that, thankfully, we could be in California within twenty-four hours if we ever needed to be. It was only after we walked down the long hall to the main exit that I realized both Kim and I were crying.

The dream that began months, maybe years, ago now seemed to have a life of its own, though on that late spring day, California was making it difficult to leave. Everywhere, the candy-colored tulips were out, and the purple and yellow irises were in joyous bloom. Puffy white clouds climbed high against the Edward Hopper blue sky.

Riding quietly along Highway 101 in the taxi, I wondered what would be the same when I returned, and what would have completely changed. I suspected, and certainly hoped, that I would grow and change. I hoped some of the elegance and the grace of Italy would rub off on me, at least a little. I was ready to live for a year in Piemonte, in the Langhe, in my *bella* Monforte and Roddino, awash in history and rich with pleasures of today. Ready to learn new things, to experience new places, and to make a home with my husband that could help us create memories with our family and each other. The time had come. And so, as comforting as San Francisco could be, and as much as I loved our family and friends and our lives here, we were off.

CHAPTER TWELVE: 2015

MARZO

Our year in Italy began, as so many good things do, with champagne.

That cold afternoon in early March, we stepped into our new house, lights lit, heat on, windows, doors, roof, walls, all beautifully in place, and Zef greeted my husband and me with house keys and glasses of bubbling Alta Langa Brut. But even before I took a sip, I felt lightheaded, frozen in place. I looked up, and up, at the soaring timbered ceiling and the cascading chandelier hanging down from it, then looked at Zef who was beaming at us.

"*Benvenuti a casa!*" he said. Welcome home.

The transformation from a dilapidated stable to a proper, respectable home was difficult for me to even process. I had never before felt such love swelling in my heart for an inanimate object, and only a few times before for a handful of precious human beings.

"*Che bella!*" I finally uttered, though it sounded inadequate. I could not find a better word in English either. It was simply overwhelming.

The roof was high. Very high. Maybe too high, as Zef and I both laughed. But since it was supported by that splendid old wall with the symphony of rock, stones, and the decades of stories they told, of the people who had lived and died here, of their loves and heartaches throughout the years, the extraordinary height was warranted. The living room, on all four sides with stones and stucco, and the grand window to the west, was everything I could have hoped them to be. The glass and wrought iron stairway that Kim had painstakingly engineered for hours on end was more like a piece of sculpture than a means of getting from one floor to the next. It was graceful, strong, functional, and witty all at once. And the kitchen, though not large, was perfect, ample, and well organized.

I finally exhaled, took a deep drink of my champagne, and laughed again while wiping away the tears. Zef presented us with a pile of gifts from himself and his wife stacked up on the kitchen counter. A case of Dolcetto wine, an entire set of plates and dishes, little espresso coffee cups, and a serving tray to hold them. But really, the present was already surrounding us.

I walked up the stairs, fingering the smoky gray wrought iron railings, cool and roughly textured. I stepped, hesitantly at first, onto each nubby glass step, surprised at how sure each one felt beneath my feet. I almost floated along the elevated glass hallway and then, for the first time, actually stood in my room, the former hayloft. The cobwebs, bugs, rusted nails, and rickety ladders had scared me off before, but now here was this welcoming room with rich brown wooden floors, stucco walls, and that same vaulted ceiling. At last I could see the view that I would be waking up to every day, stretching from my feet to the snow-covered Monviso, starkly clear and close on this frosty spring day.

Room by room, I explored the meandering house, still a little breathless from the reality of it. The bedrooms, while not large, were each comfortable and filled with light and unending views. The upstairs bedrooms had the original stone walls and the high-pitched roof, which gave them a lofty elegance. And the guest bedroom downstairs had clean, sleek lines and wonderful views of the mountains.

Even the powder room, the tiny bathroom in the hallway, tugged on my heart. The hand-stained octagonal cement tiles that Allie had discovered in the dirt behind the barn fit exactly into the four-by-six-foot space. The little room could not have looked more perfect if we had created the tiles to order.

But the most remarkable transformation was the cantina. A sloppy, treacherous underground grotto before, it was now dry and welcoming, the ideal space to sit and drink coffee or aperitivi or even enjoy a leisurely dinner. Zef had lined the floor with faded old terra-cotta tiles. Kim stands six foot five, and his three sons tower three and four inches above him, but the long central area under the arched vaulted ceilings was just high enough for any one of them to walk beneath without ducking or hitting their heads, if, that is, they stay to the middle of the room. Windows at shoulder height gave light and fresh air to a space that had been eerily dark and claustrophobic. And, as if the room needed more character, there was a series of rusty and bent old iron hooks stuck into the ceiling, ready to hang salamis or tie up a cow, should we become so inspired. But I preferred to imagine enjoying lively evenings with friends or quiet summer mornings immersed in a good book.

At last. Here it was, our house in Italy. Done. Well, sort of.

Missing still was the proverbial kitchen sink, literally. And without a sink, cooking would be impossible. There was no land-scaping at all, and the thick, sticky mud came right up to the front stoop so coming in and out all day would be a mess. It was obvious that there would be some weeks more at Casa Piccola before we could actually move into our house. Critical interior and exterior work needed to be done, and our car and the small crate with our belongings and our bed still needed to arrive from America. But it was all wonderfully close.

Maybe it was the bubbles, but as we drank our champagne, something suddenly became very clear.

Leaning against the brand-new counter in our kitchen, champagne glass in hand, Kim turned to me and said, "Think about it. How many times in our lives will we ever have an opportunity like this? We are in Italy. For a full year. We have work to do, sure, but it won't take all day, every day. We can explore Turin and Milan, maybe even Venice. We can take Italian lessons and become proficient, maybe, or at least better able to communicate. Let's go wine tasting and learn all about the wines here. Let's learn to make pasta, even *plin*. We can make it like a working vacation."

He was exactly right. I, too, wanted to embrace every moment of our "year abroad." Toasting him with a clink, I agreed with him. We continued basking in those first moments in our home, talking with Zef, exploring every nook, finding new angles and vistas to delight in. And as our glasses emptied, Kim and I began to plan. We decided that while Zef and his team worked on the remaining finishes, we would focus on truly being here, on going about our daily life with serious playfulness, discovering and learning about the Langhe, while trying to improve our Italian and our understanding of this amazing country. It was such an opportunity, such a gift. I looked forward to welcoming each new season, each holiday, familiar or not, and maybe even trying to become a part of this beguiling little community.

From that day on, the Langhe began to seem different to me because it was where I really lived. No longer a visitor or tourist, this was my home.

I loved the idea that my drive to the grocery store was a meandering four-mile trek through hazelnut orchards into the town of Dogliani, and that the bank was right at the piazza in Monforte, requiring a coffee before and after every visit, which pretty much took up our morning. I loved that every day I needed new words, like hairdresser (*parrucchieri*) and butcher shop (*macelleria*) and hundreds more, like bed sheets (*lenzuola*), napkins, and tablecloth (these are really hard: *tovaglioli e tovaglia*) although I still do not know the one for that folding clothes-drying rack. The verb *imparare* (to learn) was almost impossible for me to master, although Lord knows I needed it. But I was starting to be comfortable actually using some verbs in sentences. Sometimes I would rearrange the sentence to use words I did know, and sometimes I would say something else entirely. It almost did not matter. I was starting to have halting conversations with people, which was exhilarating.

I loved the unapologetically non-secular nature of this beautiful country. It is part of what makes it feel so Italian. Nearly all Italians identify as Catholic, and the presence of the Holy Roman Catholic Church is everywhere. There are crucifixes on the post office walls as well as in the police stations and all the hospitals. Every few miles along the back roads is a shrine to Saint Mary and the Holy Family, with complex, emotional frescoes often with flowers, real and plastic, placed at the Virgin's feet. I wondered about the stories behind each of these, whose heart was broken, whose love lives on.

With Catholicism so prevalent, it is no surprise that many of the holidays in Italy are also religious. We arrived here just at the end of Carnevale, before the beginning of Lent, in time to catch all of the *bugie* in the markets and *panifici*. These are light, crispy strips of dough, like flaky, sweet tortilla chips, fried and covered with clouds of powdered sugar. I saw them everywhere, and was finally compelled to buy a white paper bag or two filled with them. I bit into one and the sugar flew up my nose and onto my face as I ate; good, but more sweet than satisfying. I brought the rest to the construction site and the workers happily passed them around, laughing and devouring them in an instant. The pastries clearly evoked all kinds of memories for these men, if not yet for me.

It was one day that same March that we first encountered the unforgettable Nicoletta. She is the owner, chef, and joy of Trattoria dell'Amicizia, which is less than a kilometer from our house, right at the heart of our commune of Roddino. With all the travel back and forth between Italy and the States that past year, my stomach was in a delicate condition. Or maybe it was the bugie. I am not actually allergic to anything except chives, but it suddenly seemed like I was sensitive to everything—meat, milk, wheat, uncooked veggies, you name it. When Julia and Paul Child first lived in Paris, they referred to this condition as being "bilious," the uncomfortable way their stomachs sometimes felt while adapting to a whole new diet. I was not 100 percent sure of the true diagnosis, but "bilious" sure sounded like how I was feeling.

So when we walked into Nicoletta's Trattoria dell'Amicizia for lunch that day, the restaurant on Roddino's main road that we had passed by a hundred times before, I had already decided I really could not eat anything. My husband ordered the worker's lunch, and I told the nice woman from the trattoria that, unfortunately, I really did not feel like eating anything at that moment.

"Nothing??? Maybe just some *Vitello al Barolo*?" she asked in English. I declined as gracefully as I could but Nicoletta is not one to walk away from a challenge. "Maybe you don't eat meat. How about just a plate of *tajarin*, pasta, with tomato sauce? Or roasted eggplant?" I was not sure how heavy either of those would be, so I declined again. Rather than being insulted, like some chefs would have been, she pulled up a chair. "Tell me what you CAN eat." She was so sweet, and curious, her big green eyes looking at me sympathetically, as if coaxing a child. "How about anchovies in parsley sauce?" She was winning me over.

"Well, do you have something simple, like a chicken breast?" I asked. Very few restaurants serve chicken in the Langhe, and the people there cannot comprehend why it is ubiquitous in American restaurants. So, of course, she did not have chicken.

"Okay. Maybe . . . cheese?"

Nicoletta brightened. "Cheese!! *Formaggio! Certo!* Maybe a little cooked vegetables on the side? *Pepperoni Agrodolce*—sweet and sour peppers?" She really was so kind, and so not at all put off by my fussiness, that her warmth melted me.

"Okay," I said. "Maybe a small plate."

Delighted, Nicoletta arrived shortly with my husband's three-course lunch, with wine, of course, and my beautifully arranged plate with slices of Parmesan, mozzarella, and Toma cheeses, perfectly roasted red and yellow peppers, very lightly dressed in sweet and sour vinaigrette, a basket of bread and breadsticks, and a glass of cold water. It was actually a perfect lunch for each of us. I left, comfortably full, feeling settled and so nurtured. To me, that is the essence of truly great cooking—it is not about spectacle or pretense, but about simply caring for someone else. Italians understand this. As does Nicoletta.

✳✳✳*Pepperoni Agrodolce*✳✳✳

4–5 large red and yellow sweet peppers
¼ cup of olive oil
1 garlic clove
Salt and pepper
2 tablespoons of sugar
½ cup white wine vinegar
½ cup of good olives, pitted
¼ cup salt capers, rinsed

Wash the peppers, slice them lengthwise, and remove their seeds and white pith.

In a large sauté pan over moderate heat, add the olive oil. Lightly smash and peel the garlic clove, and add it to the oil for about 1 minute, just long enough to flavor the oil but not long enough for it to brown. Then remove the clove and discard it.

Add the peppers to the oil, stirring frequently, for about 5 or 6 minutes. Season lightly with salt and pepper. Turn the heat down a notch.

Combine the sugar and the vinegar, stir, then add the liquid to the peppers, and cook over low heat for another 5 or 6 minutes until the peppers start to soften. Still stirring frequently, add the olives and capers and cook for about 10 more minutes, until the peppers are soft and all the flavors have blended nicely. Serve as a side dish, a starter, or as a topping for slices of grilled bread.

APRILE

The first big holiday we celebrated as unofficial Italian residents was Easter, *Pasqua*. It came that year in early April, as the weather was just beginning to warm and the grapevines were about ready to burst out in green. Easter Sunday in Italy is in some ways more important than Christmas. It is followed by Easter Monday, or *Pasquetta*, when families go out for an hours-long luncheon feast and kids receive eggs as big as they are, filled with toys. Between the various Masses, dinners, lunches, days off from work, and toys for the kids, it is a wonderful holiday, and, of course, it is a harbinger of spring, putting everyone in a celebratory mood.

Growing up in the fifties and sixties in California's Santa Clara Valley, Easter was always somehow kind of disappointing for me. I remember Easter frocks that were scratchy and stiff, and polished new shoes that pinched my feet. As I grew older, the Easter school vacation week seemed to always be frustratingly chilly or rainy. We were all ready for warm weather and the freedom that would bring, but so often we sat at Easter Mass in our little chiffon dresses, freezing in the pews, or covered up with winter coats. As an adult, the holiday just made me yearn for the children I never was able to have, and more recently, for the sweet parents I had just lost, raw with memories of pastel-colored jelly beans and silly hiding places and the family traditions that were part of such an innocent time long ago. The sense of melancholy I felt at Easter was always in gloomy contrast to the flurry of new life budding forth around me.

On this Easter Sunday morning, my husband suggested we drive down to the sea in Liguria, taking the back roads, called the Napoleonic Trail, that runs along the hilltops almost as far as Savona. It is like driving through a national park, unspoiled and glorious. One hour and a half later, when we reached the beaches, we saw people milling about, but they were not a summer-type crowd. Rather, they were families out to lunch, parents, grandparents, and children cradling their giant eggs while trying to peer into them to peek at the treasures stashed inside. We found a restaurant on the beach that miraculously still had parking, which was all we really needed to lure us in. Pure white walls and high ceilings, with one glass wall between the dining room and the beach, it was elegant and the owners welcoming. We sat out on the balcony overlooking the sea and drank champagne. The breeze was cool, but the pasta was perfect, and the roast fish tasted like the ocean. I do believe it is the loveliest Easter I have ever experienced.

The weather continued to be chilly and fresh, but my husband started a new habit of riding his bike several mornings a week. I so admired that he was gone for a good hour, and came home sweaty and in a great mood. A few weeks into this, he confessed that he had been stopping at Trattoria dell'Amicizia on the way up the hill and again on the way back down, for coffee and a long chat with Nicoletta's husband, Fabio, who is the barista. Fabio did not really speak English, so my husband needed to try out his best Italian on him, starting with *"Caffè espresso macchiato, per favore"* and they would go from there. I thought it was a wonderful mix of exercise, coffee, companionship, and friendship that started our days off so beautifully.

We also made it a point every week to go to one of the other small local restaurants near Roddino, all owned and managed by families. I loved to have dinner at La Torricella, which just opened less than a year before, and now was adding nine guest rooms and a spa. Francesco is the most charming of hosts, and his wife, Alessandra, is a wonderful chef, sweet, unflappable, and inventive. Her sister, Silvia, has taken over the wine operation with gentle guidance from their father, Diego. She is part of a new generation of women winemakers in the region who are creating some exceptional vintages.

One night as Francesco was seating us, he introduced us to another couple at the next table. "These are your neighbors," he announced. "Antonio and Angela." Another Angela. I was pleased to be surrounded by angels. We decided to all sit at the same table, since Antonio spoke some English and both seemed happy to get acquainted with the new foreigners in the neighborhood, and, of course, we were eager to get to know them. Angela spoke no English, but her easy laughter communicated her essential warmth, kindness, and charm, and both new friends proved to be delightful dinner companions. Our conversation was a melange of my broken but well-meaning Italian, Antonio's translations for Angela, his fairly successful attempts at using complex sentences in English with occasional translation help from me, and Kim's charm and intelligence accentuated with a few perfect Italian words punctuating his opinions. As those that we enjoyed with Biagio and our other dear Angela, our conversation somehow seemed to flow, encouraged, of course, by great food, fine wine, and an abundance of kind intentions.

Although the house was getting closer to completion each day, it was still not habitable so we continued living at Casa Piccola. It is hard to express the simple satisfaction I felt there, monitoring the construction, while enjoying our daily interactions with Angela and Biagio who were starting to ready their massive *orto*, or vegetable garden, for the summer ahead. Every new vegetable they planted was another Italian lesson for me, as I learned *pomodori, zucche,* and *asparagi.*

Increasingly, I noticed how much in common we had with so many of the people we met, even though our backgrounds at first blush seemed to be so different. I believe that shared passions and interests cut through cultural differences, and I had seen that throughout my travels during my career in advertising. My teams in Singapore, Paris, Buenos Aires, and Tel Aviv and I often had more in common with one another than we did with many of our neighbors in our own towns. And here in the Langhe, our new neighbors shared with us a love for this unique and beautiful land, the vistas, the gentle climate. I found in them a common respect for the wines it produced, along with the truffles, veal, and hazelnuts. Fortunately, I did not need to be able to conjugate too many verbs to understand our common values. Sometimes a simple toast, a smile, or a shared meal said it all. And this gracious acceptance by Nicoletta and Fabio, Antonio and Angela, and Biagio and Angela, did more to make me love Italy than they will ever know.

With the snows all melting and the weather turning more springlike, Kim and I began finalizing landscape plans and taking steps to begin preparing the property. I could not wait to have something green growing outside, the way it was before we began construction, only a little less wild. So the next few weeks were particularly exciting, messy, dirty, and a little hectic, but also enormously satisfying.

My simple, rural life now was a far cry from the life I lived when I was navigating the rocky terrain of advertising. My blazer and black slacks hung untouched in the closet. I lived in jeans and sweatshirts. Leather flats were swapped for rubber boots and running shoes, or no shoes at all. Traipsing around the yard, I had found a new kind of stamina, and mopping the floor each day no longer left me winded. Dinners out were usually less than forty euros for the two of us, and tasted more delicious than anything we had back in the United States. Meanwhile, other luxuries like manicures and facials were no longer on my to-do list. But I was not complaining. Not one tiny bit.

MAGGIO

The first day of May here is a holiday, one of the few that is not religious. It is a day that celebrates the Italian worker, like America's Labor Day, and so it was a day that Zef's men actually did not work. That made it an exceptionally quiet day, and I was more aware than ever of the thousands of different birds chattering away in the newly green trees. With no place to go, I found it the perfect day to unpack some of our things for the house that had arrived, to place the few pieces of furniture that we had and to begin to get it settled. Even our car, oversized and American as it is, had finally come. Perhaps most importantly, our sink was now in place and our stove was working. Midway through unpacking, it occurred to my husband and me that the house was now finished enough for us to actually spend the first night in our home.

We packed up all our belongings from Casa Piccola and spent hours trying, but probably failing, to leave it as clean as we had found it. We hugged goodbye and bid *grazie* to Biagio and Angela, and as we walked the few hundred feet across their yard to ours, through our own front door, I was brimming with emotion.

Placing the clean sheets on my bed was an unexpected pleasure. As I smoothed the pillow cases and tucked in the blankets, I marveled that this was all really real. Of course, the only bathroom that was finished was the one in the downstairs guest room, so that was the room we would live in for a while, quite happily. Work would continue on the inside and the outside of the house, and I would be cleaning the floors daily, sometimes twice a day, to pick up the dirt that was constantly being tracked in. But we were finally going to be sleeping in our home.

That night I lay in bed, my muscles aching, and simply let the birds' songs carry me into a deep slumber. I woke up early the next day, and even before I opened my eyes, I felt the warm blanket over me, cool morning air on my face, Kim sleeping quietly next to me, and was overwhelmed by that rare sensation of being exactly where I was supposed to be, perfectly centered on the earth, and in my life.

Now fully ensconced in our home, the days became long and interesting. Zef and his men arrived well before eight o'clock, and over our coffee we would wave at them through the windows as they set about their work. We witnessed a giant cement truck pumping out concrete into twenty-five-foot-deep holes filled with rebar, creating pilings for the pool. We carved out a driveway and parking area in the field above the house, surrounding it with a cement retaining wall. Because we are in a UNESCO-protected area, we then had to clad the entire wall in local stone, consistent with the historic architecture of the area. Trees and bushes were being placed and planted, electricians and plumbers were connecting and disconnecting things—there was always something exciting to watch or to choose. I loved the feeling of moving forward, of finishing a project, of watching our dream take shape.

Then, with great excitement, we welcomed our son Flynn and his girlfriend, Katherine, who came to visit with Flynn's roommate from college. The three arrived laden with hiking and climbing gear, and were eager to explore the many trails of the Alps and Liguria. I fortified them as best I could for a day or two, with all the gnocchi and pasta they could eat. Then Kim drove them to Monviso for a hike and an overnight at the summit. They carried maps and compasses and had done their homework, but a late spring storm dumped two feet of snow at the seven-thousand-foot elevation, just before they arrived. The mountain was enveloped in fog and freezing rain, and when they finally found the *rifugio* where they had hoped to stay, it was completely snowed in, so they were compelled to spend an hour digging a path in the snow to a second-floor window before forcing it open. Climbing in, they spent the night there, dry, but freezing, and were just able to heat coffee in the morning over a small fire they made outside.

I never heard all the graphic details, but when Kim went to pick them up the next day, they were happy though exhausted, and in bed that night by seven. Flynn and Katherine said goodbye to their friend, then recuperated with us at home for a few days. Soon anxious for the next adventure, they rented a Vespa and trekked around Ligúria for a long weekend, spending their days climbing rocks suspended by ropes and pulleys over the sea. In the evenings, they enjoyed romantic dinners in the little medieval towns, discovering the pastas, seafood, and local wine. They returned home ebullient, rested, and nicely tanned. I marveled at what energy and agility they both had and vicariously enjoyed the thoroughly different perspective on the region they showed us. Such youth and exuberance was inspiring.

In the midst of this happy confusion, we met our other neighbors. Next door, literally attached to our house, there is a three-story home owned by an older couple who arrived from nearby Turin. Biagio and Angela introduced us to them, explaining to us that these folks, Piero and Innes, spent winters in the city, came out here to the country for the summers, and had been doing so all of their lives.

Innes is gracious, with a Sophia Loren smile, and I can imagine that she was once a beauty. Piero apologized, saying that he did not speak English, but he did speak both Italian and Piemontese. As he said this, he laughed and his blue eyes twinkled, and I discovered I adored him already. He then told us his daughter and granddaughter both speak English, and they visit often. Although Piero was in his mid-eighties and Innes was nearly ninety, they kept their apartment on the second and third floors. I was in awe as I watched them clamber up and down the exposed metal stairs several times a day. Every day except Sunday, when they went to church, they worked for hours in their large garden, slashing weeds, planting vegetables, and growing flowers that were astounding. Biagio told me that Innes and Piero were professional gardeners and had sold vegetables and flowers at the Turin farmers market for years. He clearly admired them, their spirit, and their vitality. So did I.

And on one warm Saturday in late May, Monica invited us to a soccer game featuring Monforte's respectably good home team, the Barolo Boys. She told us that her husband, Livio, was their coach. He was also the town's mayor. He was well known and well liked throughout the area since he was the person who manufactured cement stakes for the vineyards, which were sturdy, well priced, and that lasted forever.

The team's name, the Barolo Boys, is an homage to their fathers and grandfathers, the makers of the noble Barolo wine that fuels so much of Monforte's energy. During the pregame meal at Il Grappolo D'Oro in the piazza, they all enjoyed their steak and pasta, perhaps a cigarette or two, and always had ready smiles and handshakes for any of us who came to wish them well. On the field, they played with skill, passion, and irreverence. Handsome, approachable, and funny, they published a Barolo Boys calendar featuring the players in their underwear (or less), sans manscaping, while posing in and around the vineyards and wine cellars of the region. Livio did not appear in the calendar. But I assumed he was admired by his team, because during every break they boisterously sang songs about him. I had no idea what the words actually meant, but they made the crowds roar with laughter and Livio blush. When they win, which they did that perfect spring day, they hoist Livio on their shoulders and carry him off the field. It was as much fun as I have ever had at a sporting event. The young team is a testament to the new generation that carries on the spirit and soul of the Langhe.

Every day we discover anew that as beautiful, scenic, and gastronomically extraordinary as this region is, its true beauty is in its people, young and old.

GIUGNO

Now, I do need to admit that life here was not perfect. It is, after all, real. And at moments, frustrating. Like on an early June morning, when I sleepily made my way down the stairs toward the tea and coffee, and before I could clear my head with the first sip, I came upon a squirming trail of creepy little ants, marching relentlessly across the counter like Napoleon's army into Mondovi. I have never in my life had ants, except once in New Jersey when I left the honey out all night on the counter, but that episode lasted exactly one day and, in retrospect, I was asking for it. My house is not spotless, but it is clean and I take pride in that. Yet Italian ants do not care. They had found me, and they had found me with a vengeance.

And we are not talking about a few ants running in a stream out the door. We are talking about scores of them, mobilized and running across the kitchen counter one day, along the kitchen floor the next, up a stucco wall the next day, and then discovering the living room. It was like a Hitchcock movie: *The Ants*. It was maddening. I tried every safe anti-ant product I could find, and even some that are maybe not so safe. I started mopping the kitchen and dining room floor with hot sudsy water every night before bed. And nothing helped. Ants. Ants. Insidious little ants. Every damn day.

Then, one day, as suddenly as they arrived, they left. I told myself that they were here first, that, after all, this was a barn just a short time ago. And I heard from all my neighbors here in the country that they, too, have ants. But I still believe it was something personal. As lovely and welcoming and kind as the Italians have been to us, the ants were churlish and mean-spirited. Thank goodness, most everything else about the Langhe makes up for the infernal little buggers.

It was late in June, a simmering hot day, and I was clearing lunch dishes when I heard voices in the courtyard. There were two men, talking animatedly, looking at and pointing to our home. I had heard there were vagabonds in the area, who sometimes steal from the homes or pilfer through people's yards looking to snatch tools or scrap iron. Having already encountered strangers at the door once or twice at Casa Piccola, I was now alarmed at these two unfamiliar visitors. Our builders were all away on their lunch break, and my husband was working upstairs, when the two men came boldly around to the porch and peered in at me. I called up to my husband as I went to answer the door.

"*Buongiorno,*" said the younger of the two old men. He came toward me as if to enter the house, and I was taken aback at his assertiveness. Then I noticed he was wearing a clerical collar. My Lord, I realized, he was the pastor of Roddino, and he was with his eighty-five-year-old assistant. My husband appeared, prepared to protect me from all harm, and he, too, stopped short. "*Buongiorno, Padre,*" I said, hoping it was the correct thing to say, but honestly having no idea. I gestured for them to come into the house, which they did quite happily. When I asked them if they would like to sit down, they politely declined.

The good father began speaking in Italian, and within a few minutes I started to understand that he was welcoming us to our new home. He chatted about the church in Roddino and Monforte, as he was the pastor for both parishes, and wondered if I attended Mass. I said that I did, but only occasionally, and he did not seem at all troubled by my waywardness.

Then he asked if he could bless our home. I looked to my husband who nodded, and before I knew it, we were all holding hands, the four of us in our living room, saying the Lord's Prayer, they in Italian, I in English, and my husband listening attentively. The clergyman then began a short prayer, and I understood that he was wishing us health and safety in our home and that the Lord's blessing would be with us all of our days. I looked up and saw through my sudden tears that my husband was moved as well. When the prayer ended, we offered the men of God an espresso, which they declined, then I offered a small donation to the church, which they also declined. They left, pleased that they were able to simply impart God's blessing upon our new, old, too-high, and unfinished house.

As they drove away, I felt my heart in my chest, and thought now, now we were truly at home in Italy.

LUGLIO

The summer sun in the Langhe bakes you through to your bones. Lizards scamper across the hot pavement and slide underneath the floor of the house to find shade. Grapevines grow up inches overnight as the green fruit begins to clump wildly together here and there and miles of twisting tendrils cling to anything they can reach. The snow on the Alps is nearly all melted, except for one tenacious patch on the very top of Monviso. I am grateful for the light breezes that tend to drift over us in the afternoon.

All the summer heat had dried out the mucky dirt in our yard sufficiently to allow us to finish the pool, put in grass seed, and build the stone stairs from the road all the way to our front door. Our landscaping, as sparse and tentative as it was, was in.

From the first time my husband mentioned it, I was absolutely against the idea of a pool. I was adamant; it was only hot enough to swim from June through August, there was no room for a pool, and it would absolutely break our budget. But he insisted and would not listen to reason.

I could not have been more wrong.

On the really hot summer days, the pool is the one and only thing that cools me down, chilling my skin, leaving my wet hair to dry slowly throughout dinner, making me feel like I am nine years old again. On the rare days that I don't swim, merely looking at the pool is calming and it is the focal point of the yard. It has become a kind of gathering place for us and for our neighbors and their kids, splashing and laughing in the afternoon, or just sitting under the umbrella, with cold drinks in our hands, while looking at the view toward the Alps and Liguria and feeling all the better for it.

After toiling for months and months, planning, building, digging, moving in, and settling in, we were finally beginning to reap the fruits of our labors and enjoy the sweet life in Italy. Our son Kelly, Flynn's twin brother, arrived from New York for a visit, and immediately claimed the upstairs guest room as forever his. I loved his ownership of it. His room. It was just what I hoped our sons would feel about our home. Kelly would float for hours on the air mattress in the pool while reading one of his neuroscience textbooks. And that summer, at his suggestion, he and I planted night-blooming jasmine along the old wall in the garden. Tiny little sprigs, they grew swiftly and happily and remind me of him every time I see them.

From time to time, more friends and family came to visit, for a few days or even a week. We took little car trips, to France, to Germany, to other corners of Italy. It was just as I dreamed it would be.

And then, as we started to develop our routines of eating out, going for coffee, and appearing at community festas, something emerged that I had not anticipated. Friendship. *Amicizia*, like the Trattoria. We began to become friends, good, true friends, with the people who live here. Of course, there were Angela and Biagio and their sweet family, for whom we were developing a deep, abiding affection. My husband, on his daily trips for coffee at Trattoria dell'Amicizia, had by now fully befriended both Fabio and Nicoletta, so much so that we sometimes went out for pizza with them and their twins on their day off. But the big surprise came with Piero and Innes.

Piero was always quick to offer a greeting in the morning, comments about my morning walk, the weather, the plans for the day, or any number of pleasantries that we all enjoyed. The conversation was a little more awkward between him and my husband, as my husband was, well, more hesitant with his Italian. But they shared a love of bicycle riding and Piero was always enthusiastically praising my husband after any trip he took, short or long. "*Bravo!*" he would say, smiling and shaking his head in awe. And later he would say to me how he wished my husband would learn Italian so they could chat.

One day, as his own way of communicating friendship, my husband baked a loaf of his special, crusty San Francisco–type sourdough bread and brought it over to Piero, still warm from the oven. The gesture was clear in any language, and Piero was plainly touched. However, in the Langhe, people love to offer gifts. It is who they are. It is what they do.

Not to be outdone, Piero showed up at our door the next day with a loaf of bread he had baked, and a basket of green beans picked moments earlier from his garden. I'll see your bread, and raise you green beans, in essence. It was clearly Game On. Delighted with both of Piero's offerings, and taken aback by his kindness, we had to plan our response. But how could we top freshly picked produce? We had no vegetable garden, no bountiful *orto* with which to compete. So the following Monday at the Monforte farmers market, my husband went to his friends at the cheese truck and ordered a half kilo of thirty-month-old Parmigiano Reggiano, sliced fresh from their huge cheese wheel and nicely wrapped in paper. Any proper Italian could put that to good use, and it was probably one of the few items Piero and Innes used every day but did not grow themselves. The cheese was a success, and Piero thanked us profusely, as he shrewdly plotted his next maneuver.

What we had not planned for was that Innes was a cousin of Gemma, owner of Osteria Da Gemma in Roddino, our famed Roddino restaurant, the one that Italian people drive for miles just to visit, and the place where on Wednesday mornings, Gemma and her friends make the pasta, *plin* and *tajarin*, for the week ahead. And that following Wednesday, Piero knocked at our kitchen door.

I opened it to find him standing there holding a large wicker basket overflowing with fresh *tajarin*. He and Innes had just come from Da Gemma, where they had joined their neighbors in the weekly pasta making, and were able to take a little extra home, which he insisted was too much for the two of them. To the basket, Innes had added two jars of her *salsa di pomodori*, made with tomatoes from their garden, of course, and Piero with his blue eyes twinkling said, "*Buon appetito.*"

And that was it. It was priceless. He had won fair and square. We called it a truce. There was no way for us to ever top the generosity of their gift.

We continued to go about our daily activities, and as we encountered more local residents, we started to realize that everyone already knew who we were. We were "the Americans." And surprisingly, they were all willing and ready to accept us into their community, in spite of our ignorance of local customs, and our far from fluent Italian sprinkled with frequent mistakes. Having never before lived in such a small town, I have never experienced such unconditional acceptance in a community. It felt a little like I was living on a small college campus, like the one where I went to school, and any time you go out to dinner, to the store, or for coffee, you see two or three people you know, say hello, and catch up on the latest news. It is an unusual feeling. And after so many years living in big cities, it was a most welcome one.

AGOSTO

Summer gently wrapped itself around us, bringing with it a myriad of new sensations. I had sunburned shoulders for the first time in decades. We had ladybugs on all the windows in our home and I found a scorpion on the terrace. Thunder, lightning, and hailstorms blew through and cleaned the air. There were fireflies at night, and stars in constellations I had never before seen. There were fragrant lavender bushes, and fat, noisy, lazy bees in our gardens. There were fresh, cool mornings and baking hot afternoons that melted into Aperol-colored sunsets.

Many nights, we set up our grill and made the most of the beautiful Langhe veal that we saw each day in the butcher's case, searing it quickly, slicing it on the diagonal, and serving it with parsley and mint *bagnetto verde*. The veal here is so tender and juicy and perfect, unlike any meat I have ever known. Some nights, we switched up and barbecued chicken with delicately spiced sausage, or even fish, grilling as many nights as we could. Or sometimes, my husband would throw on a dozen pork ribs, cooking them until crispy and savory, and bring some over to Piero, who had said just the smell from the smoky grill gave him pleasure. A plate of something wonderful from the grill, accompanied by greens (often just pulled from one of our neighbors' gardens with soil still clinging to the roots) and sweet, meaty tomatoes from the outdoor market, smothered with virgin olive oil and a thick balsamic—that was often dinner.

On those summer nights, we started to notice that no matter how many hours Piero and Innes worked each day, no matter how hot the day might have been, they would climb into their Fiat a little before 8:00 p.m. and disappear until midnight, when we would hear them pull into the gravel driveway and climb up the stairs back home. Every single night. There is no way I could sustain that kind of social life. I wondered where they went, and what they did. And I worried a little about them, out late at night, party animals, and at their age. It was such a mystery. Yet it was just one more reason to admire them.

In Roddino, there is one wedding cake of a church perched in the center of the old town on the very top of the hill, plus four tiny chapels dotted around the area that are practically abandoned except for one day each year when the town holds an annual *festa* for it, with profits going to the upkeep of the chapel. In early August, we attended our first such festival at the chapel of San Lorenzo on the outskirts of town. Not knowing what to expect, what to do, or how to maneuver in Italian with anything more than the usual greetings or comments on the weather, we arrived early. Tents and long tables were set up in the shade of the pine trees in the fields next to the chapel. Some of the men in town had arrived that morning to prepare and light the giant grills, while others hauled in ribs, chicken, and sausage that they roasted for hours over smoldering coals. Salads of fresh Toma cheeses, anchovies in green sauce, crispy fried potatoes, bread, water, wine, and beer are on offer. For twelve euros, you can eat and drink your fill and everybody, absolutely everybody, is there. They hold five o'clock evening Mass in the diminutive San Lorenzo chapel, but most people arrive after the services, like we did, line up to buy the tickets for dinner, then line up again to have their paper plates laden with food. Thankfully, the first person we encountered amongst the crowd was our dear neighbor Angela, who led us to her table and made places for us to sit. Biagio was up near the grill, manning the drinks table, and saved me a chilled bottle of Arneis wine. Alongside my slow-cooked ribs and sausages, it was ice-cold nirvana.

Schoolchildren played games and ran in the fields for hours behind the church, while their parents and other adults, like us, sat at the communal tables and ate, drank, and chatted late into the warm evening. The moon climbed high into the sky before anyone even thought about heading for home. We were thrilled to see that we actually knew so many people, some only by sight—the nice lady from the card shop, the friendly cop, Gemma. Of course, we also greeted Innes arriving on Piero's arm, and our friends Antonio and Angela who appeared with their two beautiful children and their partners.

The legend that goes along with the Festa di San Lorenzo gives an interesting overtone to the festa. Apparently Saint Lorenzo, the original, was martyred, as so many saints were. But Lorenzo's sad fate was to be burned. He was literally roasted over a fire, and at some point said, "I am done on this side; turn me over." Now, there are Catholic scholars that will swear this tale is true. If so, he had an amazing sense of humor to go along with his unwavering faith and I admire him for both.

Regardless, the night was everything wonderful about summer, relaxed and festive. And the Festa di San Lorenzo remains far and away the highlight of our summer in Roddino, when for one evening the little town welcomes more than five hundred people into their community. I vowed to attend every year.

As the August heat lingered, the Italians began to celebrate their unique holiday of Ferragosto. Technically, August 15 is the Feast of the Assumption, which kicks off Ferragosto. But Ferragosto in reality is a moving holiday of two to four weeks, where everyone gets away to the ocean or mountains. It makes for a quiet Langhe. Stores are shuttered. Restaurants are dark. Gyms close. I once heard in a sermon that God created hot summer days so that we would slow down and listen and reflect. I find it the ideal time for taking naps in the shade while pretending to read, or for searching the night sky for shooting stars. It was also the ideal time for *Pasta alla Norma*.

Pasta alla Norma is a Sicilian dish, from Catania. Antonio and Angela, who also come from the South, cooked it for us one memorable night in late summer. They explained to us that *Pasta alla Norma* is named after the 1831 opera *Norma*, a wildly popular tour de force by Vincenzo Bellini. It was such a success and so beloved that the Catanians created a pasta in its honor. After all, what higher compliment could there be? The recipe is now beloved, too. And while there seems to be a few variations on it, there is strong agreement on five key points:

1. You must use a short, fat pasta, like a giant macaroni or a short, oversized penne. No long noodles. No linguine or spaghetti. Never.

2. You must use Ricotta Salata cheese to grate on top. Not Parmesan. Not Pecorino. There is something about the tangy creaminess of this cheese that doesn't really melt, but rather melds with the pasta, making it completely unique, uniquely Norma.

3. You can use fresh or canned tomatoes, but they must be peeled. And if you use canned, you need flavorful San Marzano plum tomatoes. Of course, canned tomatoes are never quite as good as the best seasonal, sun-ripened garden tomatoes, but they are far better than

the tasteless hothouse varieties we sometimes get in stores. And you can never use cherry tomatoes—nope, not even fresh ones.

4. The eggplant slices must be ever so gently fried in olive oil, not grilled. There is something about the light caramelizing resulting from slow, careful sautéing that tenderizes the eggplant and gives it an intense flavor. It really doesn't make it at all heavy, the way our friends cooked it, since it is actually the only oil in the dish. So fry away, gently, and do not feel guilty.

5. You cannot use fresh pasta. I have no idea why. But you can't. That's what the Catanians say. And who am I to argue with a Sicilian about pasta?

Our friends were quite proud and excited to show us how to make it, to share a little piece of their Southern Italian culture with us. When we arrived, they already had their *mise en place* neatly lined up on the counter around the stove: the freshest of eggplants, basil, two cloves of garlic, fat, chunky penne, and a bowl of Ricotta Salata. Still missing were the tomatoes, but Angela, who was smiling at me with her basket over her arm, presented me with another basket, before leading me into their orto to harvest them. Warm from the sun and gently pliable, the red fruit fell into my hand willingly, one after another, until we had enough for dinner and another basketful for us to take home afterward.

Over at the stove, Antonio, sipping his wine with one hand and stirring with the other, patiently explained to Kim, step-by-step, how to create his beloved dish.

"First salt, then pat dry, and slowly, slowly cook the *melanzane*. *Piano, piano.* Gently. Put the two garlic cloves here, on the side of the pan—not even in the oil, just near enough to perfume the air." Kim watched attentively. Antonio grated the Ricotta Salata, and handed us each a morsel of the salty cheese so we could taste the bright, lusty flavor. Meanwhile, Angela, breaking every rule of prepping vegetables that I had ever heard of, expertly peeled and chopped the tomatoes completely in her hand with a finely honed paring knife, without using a cutting board, producing perfect piece after perfect bite-sized piece. I asked her if she ever used a cutting board, and she seemed surprised. *"Ma, perché?"* What for? She had a point. And her resulting sauce was simply tomato perfection. Restaurant chefs could take a lesson from her.

That night's pasta dinner was the essence of summer itself, and for an evening, we were transported to another region of Italy. They sent us home with a sack bulging with their tomatoes, and the moon lit our way as we walked down the hill, our ears still ringing with laughter. I felt warm and nourished, inside and out. I had learned a whole new recipe, yes, but more importantly, I had learned about something that was important to them, something that had been a part of their childhoods. Angela's skill as a cook and gardener had earned my respect, and my affection for them both grew deeper. As we walked and talked, Kim and I marveled at how easily we had shared food, ideas, and time with them, language challenges aside, and we felt very lucky.

Just as we came around the corner of our driveway, at midnight and well past our bedtime, we encountered Piero and Innes getting out of their Fiat, about to climb up their stairs after another one of their evenings out. It was the perfect opportunity to probe. Casually, I asked, *"Come è andata la vostra serata?"* How was your evening?

"Meravigliosa," Piero replied. *"Siamo stati da Gemma."* They were coming from Osteria Da Gemma, at this hour? Yes, they play cards there with their friends and cousins in Roddino, and tonight Piero won, he told us jubilantly.

So that was it. Mystery solved. All this summer, every night, they were just a kilometer away, ensconced at Osteria Da Gemma, and playing cards, probably drinking coffee and perhaps savoring a glass of wine, while certainly enjoying Gemma's desserts and their friends' company. I felt instantly better knowing they were not out driving for miles on the dark, winding roads in their little car, but were somewhere close by, somewhere so nurturing, enjoying their community and family. It was yet another example of lives well lived, and a further reason to admire them.

I went up to bed thinking how wonderful it was on that lovely summer night for them to have been doing what we were doing, only with lifetime friends, while we were nearby, getting to know new ones.

Pasta alla Norma

Coarse, flaky salt
2 medium eggplants, sliced into ¼-inch rounds
8 large, fresh ripe tomatoes or 28 ounces canned San Marzanos
2 cloves of garlic, peeled and left whole
⅓ to ½ cup olive oil
A few pinches of red pepper flakes
1 pound (500 grams) best quality pasta noodles, short and fat,
    such as macaroni or penne
6 ounces Ricotta Salata, crumbled
1 cup basil leaves, chopped

Sprinkle salt over each of the eggplant slices (how much salt? Antonio says, "not too much, not too little") and set the slices aside for 30 minutes or so to draw out the water and the bitterness.

Meanwhile, make the tomato sauce. Peel and coarsely chop the tomatoes, then place in a large saucepan. Add 1 whole clove of garlic and cook with the tomatoes over medium-low heat for 10 to 20 minutes, until most of their water has cooked off and the sauce is somewhat thickened. Do not let the garlic brown.

In a large pasta pot, begin heating ample water (4 quarts or more) to which you have added a tablespoon of salt. This is so the water will be ready for you to cook the pasta, just before it is time to serve.

Next, in a deep, wide nonstick frying pan, heat the olive oil until hot, but not smoking. (The oil should be about ¼-inch deep all around.) With a paper towel, blot the eggplant slices, wiping off the water and most of the salt. Place the slices one at a time and only one layer thick *into the hot oil. Add the second clove of garlic to this pan, being careful not to brown it at all. If all the oil becomes absorbed into the slices, do not add more oil. Simply flatten the slices with a spatula to squeeze out excess oil before frying the remaining slices. Simmer gently, turning occasionally until golden brown on both sides. Working in batches, cook all of the slices and then drain on paper towels. Discard the oil and garlic clove.*

Taste the tomato sauce. Add a dash or two of red pepper flakes, if desired. Do not add salt, as the eggplant and the cheese are already salty enough. Discard the garlic clove.

Now cook the pasta in the boiling water until al dente. Drain in a colander, then pour the pasta onto a platter, top with the tomato sauce, lightly toss, and then add the eggplant slices. Sprinkle generously with the Ricotta Salata, and garnish all over with the basil. Pass additional cheese at the table.

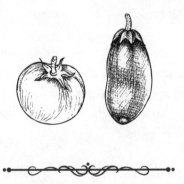

SETTEMBRE

Little by little, we started to notice that the sun was beginning to set a bit earlier, and the leaves everywhere had ever so faintly singed yellow. Fall was on its way. And in a land where vineyards hold such importance, autumn is everything. The showy colors of the harvest competed for attention with the sapphire September skies. We saw troupes of vintners, making their way through the fields, patiently sorting and selecting the bunches until each of their bright red crates was filled almost to overflowing. We remarked as the grape clusters began to disappear from the vines, first the Dolcetto, then the whites, then the Barbera, and finally the noble Nebbiolo grapes. My heart leapt when I saw the tractors rumbling through the piazza stacked high with bins of the fruit. Would it be a good harvest? A great harvest? It held so much promise.

Driving through the hills, I marveled at the bounty of the grapes. We pulled over, and I set foot on one dusty field slanting west toward the sun. The beckoning fruit was easily within my reach and I was sorely tempted to pluck a few grapes, near to bursting, just to taste the warm sweetness. But somehow, I couldn't. I felt like I would be violating someone's trust. They are so precious, each one nurtured by hand to be a living, growing sphere of possibility. No, I left them for the grape picker to harvest and send on their way to their ultimate destiny. Maybe someday, we would meet again.

In mid-September, my husband's brother, Steve, arrived in Roddino. He loves to travel. He loves wine. And I suspect he brought with him a deep curiosity for what his younger brother had been up to these past several months. Perhaps, even, he had been dispatched by the rest of the family to see what we were doing and to determine if we had completely lost our minds. There had been, after all, some spirited debate among Kim's siblings about the wisdom of us leaving the country for a full year. And we are, as we tell him, in the middle of nowhere, in Northern Italy, turning a three-hundred-year-old barn into a home. We left the familiar trappings of life in San Francisco to live in a commune in Piemonte, with beginning language skills, no connections, and no job. I could easily understand if he were on a mission to check out our sanity. I looked forward to hearing what he decided.

Steve has an agreeable way of folding into our life when he visits. He is open to everything we want to do, is eager to help with any chores we might find for him, especially in our garden, and he is charming company. He eats everything we cook, and seems to love it. He is always up for a fine dinner out, and insists on paying for at least half of everything. He is, simply, the perfect guest.

My husband's daily trips to Amicizia for coffee with Nicoletta and Fabio became Steve's routine, too. Then both brothers worked on projects in the garden until the sun lured them over to the pool. A little swimming. A little sun. Maybe a nap. Or two. Then it was time for dinner. We frequently grilled, or I would roast something for us, and every few days a trip to discover a new restaurant sounded good to all of us.

The evening sky in late summer in the town of Monforte is an ethereal neon purple glow, with church steeples backlit against it as the sun goes down late, just as the first star or planet appears. One Saturday night, Kim, Steve, and I were in the piazza finishing dinner under this radiating light when my cell phone rang. It does not ring much anymore, so I looked at it and saw it was Flynn, calling from his home in Idaho. I answered it as discreetly as I could, but he excitedly said, "Put me on speaker." I looked at Kim and Steve, and told Flynn we would call him back in two minutes, after Kim paid the check and we stepped away from the table. Out in the piazza, with Flynn now on speaker, he said, "Okay, the three of you. Tell me why Katherine and I are drinking champagne at ten in the morning here with her parents." Kim and I exchanged a look. We knew it could only be good news.

Flynn told us how, that morning, the two of them had gone for a hike with their oversized dog. When they stopped to rest, Katherine put her hand on the dog's furry neck, petting him, and found a strange little bundle tied to his collar. Flynn said he would examine it, went over to release the package, gave it to Katherine, and then got down on one knee to propose as she unwrapped the ring hidden in their dog's little bundle. She said yes, thank heavens. I cried. Then we all let out cheers. I remember looking up at the very old church on top of the hill overlooking the piazza, lit up with golden lights, against the violet sky. It was as beautiful a sight as I have ever seen.

It is quite unusual to hear English spoken here, but one day, on the morning coffee trip, my husband and Steve encountered an English-speaking gentleman named Andrew Gunn sipping an espresso at Trattoria dell'Amicizia. He is the same height as Kim, so he was hard to miss, and Nicoletta provided the introduction. Andrew explained that he had just bought a small apartment up the street in Roddino across from Osteria Da Gemma. He and his wife, Rozy, own a winery in South Africa. They bought the pied-à-terre so that they could come to the Langhe during their offseason as a kind of working vacation, enjoying and learning about the wines of our region. Right then and there, Andrew invited the men to a wine tasting he was attending later that day. After chores and naps, the three headed out. Nearly four hours later, my husband and Steve returned home with five cases of wine. It turns out, they had a good time. And the experience cemented the beginning of a new friendship. It was also the start of Steve's new favorite pastime (which, by the way, has become one of ours, too), tasting and collecting Langhe wines.

Fortunately, our cantina is large enough to accommodate this new pastime, although storing, cataloging, and protecting the bottles can be a little unwieldy. I leave the task entirely to my husband, since most days I am thoroughly happy to drink the grocery store varietal Arneis at four euros a bottle, while he enjoys stocking and pulling out different vintages for different occasions. Within a few days, Kim and Steve had carved out a corner of the cantina with Steve's name on it, containing a fine collection of Barberas, Nebbiolos, and Barolos. As a birthday tradition, we have also set up corners for Cooper and Allie, Kelly, and Flynn, the latter of which we now relabeled Flynn and Katherine. Kim's mission is to stock each section with cases of Barolo and Barbera that will be ready for them to drink long after we are not around. I hope that when they finally open a well-aged Barolo, someday in the distant future, perhaps while celebrating one of their children's weddings, they will think of us.

As for the near future—say, next week—my birthday was coming, and it was a pretty notable one, so I had asked for something special. Remembering the visit Flynn and Katherine made to Monviso in spring, I decided I wanted to go back and spend the night at its rustic rifugio at the top of the mountain. Something was calling to me to witness dawn from that vantage point and survey my world from there. I called the inn and discovered that the end of their season would be in just a few days, so we booked two rooms for the three of us and made plans for the trek back up the mountain, just before they closed.

The weather turned noticeably cooler, even as we drove the hour and a half up to Crissolo, the last little town before the rifugio. The final mile or two up to the rifugio is a goat track, literally, and

I pray we never meet a car coming back down. There are moments where I honestly have to close my eyes as our wide American car squeezes past the jagged mountain on one side, skimming the very edge of the cliff on the other. (Fortunately, Kim is driving and swears he does not close his.) Along the way are one or two shrines to those who have lost their lives on this road, which does not add to my confidence.

But after inching along for twenty minutes or so, we arrived at the inn. Low clouds obscured the actual mountain peak, and it was showering, but it didn't matter to me. Reaching for our hooded sweatshirts and warm jackets, we climbed out of the car to stretch our legs. The park was empty except for the three of us, two other sodden hikers coming down from the mountain, and off in the distance a herd of cows calmly munching the long grasses. Just walking around the meadows and trails in the mist was invigorating.

Refreshed, we climbed up the stone stairs to the rifugio to check in. The lobby was also a bar, coffeehouse, and small restaurant, and there were a few guests just finishing a late lunch or very early dinner, I wasn't sure which. The walls were pasted with faded photographs of hikers and adventurers in the snow, rain, and sun, all conquering Monviso in their own way, looking happy and weathered. There were a few well-worn maps tacked to the wall, for amateurs like us. We stood awkwardly at the bar, until one of the waitresses asked us if she could help, and we announced that we had reserved rooms for the night. She put down her tray and led us up a flight of narrow wooden stairs. We walked down a hall past the open doors of about forty empty rooms, mostly dormitory style, except for one corner room with a double bed, a crib, and a dresser, and several windows overlooking the incredible view. We continued walking. Along the narrow hallway were bedsheets hanging to dry, and we had to weave through them to find our way to the end of this maze where she showed us our two rooms. "These will be the warmest places in the hotel tonight, since they are above the cafe. There is no heat," she explained with a mix of Italian, English, and pantomime. "Dinner will be at eighteen hundred, and is included," she added.

One room had about nine single wooden beds, each with a thin mattress and a pile of woolen army blankets folded on top. The other room had about twelve single wooden beds, all dressed in the same manner. Steve took the first room, and Kim and I took the second. She gave us each a set of sheets and a pillow, so we set about putting them on our respective beds. There was one bathroom with a shower that we shared, a few steps away down the hall. Our room had one small window.

I felt like I was at camp, and I thoroughly loved it.

While I washed up, the men decided to go down to the bar for a whiskey or perhaps two. *So much for camp*, I thought.

Downstairs, Steve and my husband were having a great chat with the bartender/owner who spoke no English, while pointing to maps and photos of the mountain and enjoying their whiskeys immensely. Steve, quite at home in fine hotels and restaurants, proved gracious enough to appreciate the very simple charms of this inn, as well. As I joined them at the bar, I was once again grateful that he is so good-natured.

The waitress invited us to our table and placed a menu in front of us. "Tonight we are serving polenta," she explained. In fact, every night they serve polenta, and only polenta. But their polenta, just like the polenta in Crissolo, comes with a dozen different toppings, cheeses, ragus, a pesto, dilled sour cream, arugula, a sweet berry compote, and a giant basket of bread. As you might expect, the polenta was excellent, buttery and creamy, and we were all quite happily eating when the owner arrived and gestured to Kim to follow him. He brought my husband around behind the bar and showed him how to turn off the lights and close up for the night. He and the two waitresses were leaving. Outside, the showers had turned to a freezing rain; they lived twenty miles down the hill and were anxious to make their way down the narrow, icy road. As we were finishing our meals, they waved goodbye and locked the door to the massive hotel. On a dark, rainy night, at ten thousand feet, with the nearest human being six miles away, we were on our own.

At this point in the evening, we were the only ones left in the restaurant, and indeed, the inn. We had the entire bar and all the rooms to ourselves. I was more than a little insulted that they trusted us here alone, and were not concerned that we might empty out the bar and trash the place. Why don't we just show them how we can party?! we said. But then, it was already nearly eight o'clock and we were pretty tired, so we went upstairs to our rooms and went to bed. Dressed in two pairs of socks, my flannel nightgown, my parka, and every one of the blankets they had placed on my twin bed, I fell fast asleep in the cold, dark silence with a smile on my face. While this was not the night in a snowstorm that Flynn and Katherine had weathered, the rifugio was certainly a far cry from any of those well-appointed hotels I had frequented when I was traveling for work.

The next morning, as the sun was just beginning to spread light across the mountain, I awoke to a playful jangling of cowbells and soft lowing from the animals meandering down the hill outside of my window at the gentle insistence of their shepherd. I looked across the room at my husband who was just waking up, too, and smiled again. I changed into my jeans and warm sweater and made my way downstairs to the smell of coffee. The owner had returned and was preparing for his last day of work for the season.

I stepped outside to discover the rain was gone and the sky had cleared. Over my shoulder towered the magnificent peak of Monviso, still with a small blanket of snow on the very tip-top, and I walked through the damp meadow. Cows stepped lazily through the damp grasses, eating their breakfast as they went, clanging away, unconcerned about me. I stopped, perched on one small hill, and looked out toward the Langhe in the distance. I tried to determine where our house must be, miles away. It still felt a little like a dream.

But I was very much awake, rested, and feeling that this was a very happy birthday.

Steve, true to his quiet nature, never told us directly that he approved of our decision to build a home here, but he spent the last week with us, looking at possible houses nearby for himself. And when he returned home, he called all of Kim's siblings and cousins and suggested a family reunion for next year. At our place in Italy.

OTTOBRE

A ll around us, the autumn colors arrived in earnest. Without fruit, the leaves of the vines were a kaleidoscope of golds, burgundies, persimmons, and copper, to my delight, and the longer shadows made for sunsets like Impressionist paintings. This is my favorite time of year, and I think it is the best time to travel. Tourists are largely gone, although there are cyclists out in force, and the sun beats warm on my back when I am outside, while the house stays cool.

When you are arriving from the United States, Monforte, Roddino, and the Langhe really do feel like the middle of nowhere, so anyone who comes here has to make a concerted effort. I am always touched when a friend makes the overnight flight to Milan and the long and winding ride from the airport just to see us. We have no Eiffel Tower to climb. No Colosseum to tour. No Empire State Building. But for those who are open to it, we do offer the charms and the gastronomy unique to this region, along with friendship, a comfortable bed, and some delicious wine.

That October, our friends from Park City, Ray and Jane, came to visit for a few days, and we ate and drank and biked around like teenagers. And as they were set to leave, we decided to go with them into Monforte for one last coffee. While we were sipping and chatting at Grappolo D'Oro, a tour bus pulled up and parked nearby, and a dozen or more German tourists filed out and sat down at the table next to us. After a time, one of the ladies in their group began to sing. Loudly and clearly. It was a lilting folk song, with yodels and trills, and her voice was strong and as clear as an angel's. We looked at one another, quizzically. Suddenly, two more women joined her, harmonizing, then a few men, and within minutes it seemed the whole piazza was filled with song, in perfect harmony. It was a German flash mob of musicians who felt inspired to burst into song in the piazza that autumn morning, and leave us shivering with goose bumps. As we walked our friends to their car, marveling at what we had just experienced, we heard still more music. A horn, haunting, low and slow, echoing out from the old church. We ventured in and saw another member of the troupe, playing an ancient wooden bugle at least thirty feet long, in the middle of the center aisle. The acoustics were such that the music reverberated and seemed to be coming from heaven. I have no idea who these people were, or what songs they shared with us, but it was an otherworldly sound I will never forget.

And finally, to end the season, once again Rob and Carolyn arrived. Of course, we started at Trattoria dell'Amicizia under Nicoletta's guidance for dinner, and Kim and Rob went back daily for coffee. We visited Silvia and toasted with wine at the Barolo Bar. We splurged on dinner at Trattoria della Posta one night. We cooked. We played bridge, with me under Rob's gentle tutelage and Carolyn's infinite patience. We took drives to explore nearby towns, to see churches, or meander through ruins. Rob and my husband spent hours measuring off our outer buildings and making plans for restoring them. Carolyn and I went to town and looked for lamps, or sweets, or wine or chicken, or just strolled through the old town. We talked for hours, or read in comfortable silence. And we took naps whenever so inspired. It was easy and therapeutic and fun. They were a part of helping to shape this house from the start and I think they feel as at home here as we do.

One evening after dinner, my brain was too weary to play bridge, so the four of us took a walk up to Trattoria dell'Amicizia for an after-dinner drink, a grappa or a coffee. A wave of light and warmth and cigarette smoke engulfed us as we opened the door, and not Nicoletta, but her father, Angelo, was behind the bar to greet us. "*Ciao. Nicoletta e nella cucina*," he explained. The pub felt totally different, with dozens of locals at tables of four playing cards in the back, none of them younger than seventy. They turned to look briefly at us, then went back to their hands. We were but a brief diversion.

Angelo poured our drinks and we took them to the one vacant table and sat down. There was an abandoned deck of cards, neatly stacked and waiting for us.

Not one to turn down a playing opportunity, Rob picked them up and said, "Shall we?"

He gave them a quick shuffle and expertly dealt them out.

"What the hell?" Kim said. "What are these?"

This was a deck of cards used in Piemonte, and maybe nowhere else. There were no hearts or diamonds, nothing familiar. Only incomprehensible pictures of what might have been suits, maybe, elaborate drawings of colorful urns, swords, strange wooden logs, or were they salamis? Reassuringly, we recognized some royal figures, perhaps a queen or king, some on horseback, and a whole raft of shiny buttons. Buttons?? Some were arranged in groups of one, two, three, and so on, but seven was the highest number in the deck. Beyond that was a community of strange characters, indecipherable to us, even to Rob and Carolyn.

Carolyn counted the cards. There were fifty-two. "Well, let's try a hand anyway," she said. So we played.

What followed was a strange version of hearts, without hearts, of course, as Carolyn dealt out thirteen cards to each of us. We tried taking tricks based on what we guessed to be the highest, like face cards, or ones with more objects, although no one had a clue which suit trumped another. Does the five of salami trump the five of urns? It seemed like it should. But what about the five of buttons? They were certainly gold and shiny. As the game wore on, it got sillier and sillier. Finally, Carolyn triumphantly took the last trick as Kim cried, "YOU had the King of Buttons??!!" He was indignant, everyone else was laughing, and I was so secretly pleased that, in all the years of knowing these bridge experts, we finally played one game where they were as confused as I was.

Driving back from the airport after saying goodbye to Rob and Carolyn, our final guests of the year, Kim and I talked about how great it was to have the kind of friends who were willing to share this ride with us. Our home, I now realized, had become not just a home; it was a home in Italy. People are drawn to it—some people, anyway—and we reap the benefits. It is big enough for guests; in fact, we designed it to try and make guests as comfortable as possible, with American-sized showers and beds, a cantina, and a living room that is a cozy size for gathering. And other than the continuously dicey internet and telephone connections, or the occasional blitz from a squadron of ants, it seemed to be working as planned.

We still were not done. We had more outdoor spaces to finish and the landscaping was rudimentary and needed time to grow. And there was a whole separate section of the house that still needed to be completed.

But even in the months that we had been here, we had created some precious memories that made the effort of creating this house so worth it. Memories of family, friends, and, of course, of *amicizia*.

NOVEMBRE

The first of November, All Saints' Day, is a day to visit church and the town cemetery to honor those souls who have gone before us, parents, grandparents, loved ones. It is more of a touching and almost somber holiday, not at all like our Halloween, which I find is more about kids and twenty-somethings high on sugar and costumes. Here, you may see the occasional ghost or pumpkin, and schoolkids might have parties on October 31 since November 1 is a day off from school. But mostly it is a quiet, pensive holiday, and with leaves off the trees and the vineyards, and frost on the ground, you can almost feel the winter snows blowing across the ridges.

As the grape harvest winds down, the weather becomes quite chilly and foggy, and the talk turns to not just wine, but also to truffles. We still might find some of the winemakers sitting around big tables in the local restaurants in their flannels and mud-splattered jeans, sharing tales of this year's harvest as they refortify themselves over a hearty dinner. But in the dark of the night we could also hear the truffle hunters calling to their dogs in the valley below our home as they ferret out their harvest, hoping for a prize white truffle, or two or three. And in Monforte and in nearby Alba, we began to see men and women in elegant attire ordering *tajarin* with white truffle shaved on top, drinking glasses of ruby-colored Barolo alongside it.

Both crops have a dynamic impact on the economy and culture, and it is a wonderful time to be in the Langhe.

One clear, cool morning in early November, I was returning from my walk when I noticed a rusted green Fiat parked at the top of my driveway. There was a weathered old man at the wheel and a furry white dog in the back seat, with his head out the window looking at me, tail wagging vigorously. The duo startled me, but I nodded at them as I passed and the man leaned out his window and said, "*Buondì*," Piemontese dialect for "hi."

It was one of the three words I knew in Piemontese, so I replied, "*Buondì*." The way I pronounced it must not have impressed him much, because he switched to textbook Italian and asked me if I lived here. I was a bit taken aback, but not really threatened by the elfin little character, so I told him that I did live here, and then he said, "*Ahhh, sei americana.*"

"Yes," I said. "I am American, but I really do live here." He said he knew the house as Emma's house, the woman who lived there before us, which was not really surprising as he appeared to be well into his eighties. He told me he lived in Roddino, across from the church, in the house with all the geraniums on the balconies, which everyone in town knew well. He said he was Aurelio, a truffle hunter, a *tartufaio*, so I asked if he knew if there were truffles in the valley below our house. Oh, yes, he said, there were. But he hadn't looked for them yet, perhaps in a few weeks. His blue eyes were lively as he said maybe he would bring me some truffles when he found them. "*Molto bene, grazie!*" I replied and headed down my driveway into my yard. It was only after I walked in my door that I realized he was actually flirting with me. Honestly. That rascal! I couldn't help but smile.

Then on Friday the thirteenth, our bucolic world was shattered by news of a hateful terror attack in Paris. Along with the rest of the world, we heard about and mourned the 129 people killed, people who had been out enjoying life, dancing, watching sports, sitting at restaurants with friends, having a beer at a pub. People like me. People like you. Living here in Piemonte, the events felt chillingly close. We watched the coverage of the attacks on TV for a few days, wondering how we could possibly help. Memories of 9/11 flooded back. I was in Lower Manhattan on that surreal day in 2001, at my advertising agency on Hudson Street, and watched in stunned silence from a colleague's window as the first tower burned. And then I spied the second plane as it approached the second tower, went behind it for a beat or two, and emerged from it as an exploding fireball. I remembered the sad mental fog we experienced afterward, while trying to live our lives again. The only thing that seemed to heal us was when we could start to do something familiar again—to go back to the office, to a restaurant, board a plane—something that signaled normalcy. I felt touched that this tragedy in the country next door had not been a direct hit on our world in the Langhe, but as always, I tried to remember to stop and appreciate my loved ones, and to be grateful for the life that I had. Kim and I vowed to visit Paris again, soon, to support the people and show admiration for the incredibly beautiful City of Lights.

For me, the poignancy of the events lent even more meaning to the upcoming Thanksgiving celebration. Under their shadow, even the smallest decision seemed to take on a deeper meaning, both tender and bittersweet. Thanksgiving has always been my favorite holiday, but under any circumstances, it demands some creativity and improvisation when celebrated in a foreign country. So we set about trying to seek out the appropriate, quintessentially American ingredients, where possible.

Earlier that year, we had the good fortune to have met an extraordinarily gracious couple, Susan and B., who had a home in Monforte, and one in Washington DC, dividing their time between the two. When we heard they would be in Italy that November, we invited them to our new home for the celebration. Susan, raised in Texas, fully understood the importance of a pecan pie as part of any Thanksgiving dinner, and a few days before the big day, stopped by with a giant bag of shelled pecans and a bottle of dark Karo syrup. She might as well have been bearing gold, frankincense, and myrrh. Impossible to find anywhere in Italy, these were the key ingredients to my mom's pecan pie recipe, and really all I needed to commemorate the day. Whenever I make it, I feel my mom next to me as I bake, and it singularly makes my holiday complete.

As for the main event, we were somewhat derailed by the distinct absence of whole turkeys in the farmers markets and supermarket. We drove into the neighboring town of Dogliani and visited the *Polleria*, which specializes in chicken, and asked if they had turkeys. They said they do not, as a rule, but could indeed get one for us, if we ordered one well in advance. They were quite excited, since they had heard about this American holiday of gratitude featuring turkeys, but they had never actually been a part of one. On Wednesday before the big day, when we came to pick up the turkey, they literally ran to the back of the shop to get the bird as soon as we pulled into their parking area. They were proud and thrilled, and just possibly relieved that we had actually come to claim it. The turkey sat on the counter as we entered the shop, untrussed and awkward. The shopkeeper weighed the bird, all seven kilos of it, and wrapped it in white paper over and over, fastening the bundle of joy with tape.

Once we got the bird home, we lugged it awkwardly into the kitchen, and marveled that it took up most of our sink, sitting there like a headless Humpty Dumpty. The only way it would fit into our tiny European oven was to jam in its legs and elbows against the four sides of the oven. We set the oven thermometer for 175 degrees Celsius, planned dinner for four hours later, and hoped for the best.

Two hours later, just as we were beginning to smell that familiar aroma of Thanksgiving Day, we checked the bird. The breast meat measured 165 degrees Fahrenheit, with a toasted golden brown skin, and we realized the bird was fully cooked in nearly half the time we had calculated. Fine. We covered the bird with aluminum foil, and the minute Susan and B. arrived, we opened the champagne and began the celebration!

Champagne glasses in hand, we mashed potatoes, boiled the baby peas, made gravy, and opened the single can of cranberry sauce that our son Kelly had generously smuggled in his suitcase for us last summer. With the candles on our old wooden table lit, and the fire crackling away in the fireplace, we celebrated Thanksgiving in our new home, in our new country, with our new friends, gratefully. And it was the most delicious turkey I have ever cooked.

The following week, we ventured out on a short getaway, one we had planned months earlier to celebrate our wedding anniversary. We drove to Venice. Even saying the words "Let's drive to Venice!" gave me a thrill. The thought that we could actually get to someplace as amazing as Venice in just a few hours by car still astounds me. And at that time of the year, tourists were scarce, except for the two of us. It was wet and cold, to be sure, and the wind blew across the vaporetto that took us from the parking lot along the water to Piazza San Marco. But it just made it all the more romantic. We bumped our suitcases up and down over the bridges that span the canals, and finally found our little hotel tucked into a corner not far from the Piazza, but still out of the way. Our hotel, draped everywhere in red velvet, was fun, quaint, and surprisingly comfortable for the low offseason prices we were paying. Our room had a tiny window that looked down on a canal and over the rooftops of Venice, where seagulls put on a daily show for us. It was just the change of scene we wanted.

In the lobby was a sign for a Vivaldi concert at a nearby church, so we booked two tickets for the next night. We had dinner in a little piazza across from the church, and I happily feasted on a perfectly roasted whole fish while my husband, almost accidentally (pointing to another table and saying, "I would like that!"), ordered a superb dish of garlicky mussels covered in a delicately crunchy pizza crust. He still dreams about it. The concert was unforgettable, performed by an ensemble of twelve string musicians, and the acoustics in the old marble structure resounded perfectly. The music awakened some joyful childhood memory inside me, some perfect, peaceful, innocent time when security was pure and a given. I fell asleep to celestial notes of Vivaldi as the reverberations continued in my dreams.

✳✳✳*My Mom's Perfect Pecan Pie*✳✳✳

1 and ¾ cup sugar
¼ cup dark corn syrup (not light corn syrup!)
½ stick of butter (1/4 cup)
1 teaspoon vanilla
¼ teaspoon salt
3 eggs
1 generous cup chopped pecans
1 9-inch unbaked pastry shell in pie pan

In a saucepan over medium heat, melt butter. Add sugar and dark corn syrup and, stirring constantly, bring to boiling point for a couple of minutes.

Take pan off stove and add vanilla and salt. Cool slightly. Meanwhile, in a large mixing bowl, beat eggs lightly. Very, very gradually, add warm sugar mixture to eggs, being careful eggs don't cook. Blend well with a whisk. Then add pecans and stir until blended.

Pour mixture into unbaked pie crust. Place on cookie sheet and bake at 350 degrees Fahrenheit for 35 to 40 minutes, or just until filling is set and no longer jiggles.

DECEMBRE

Back home in Roddino again, soups, stews, and big wood fires sustained us through this dark, chilly season. My morning walks were distinctly cold, quite different from the rest of the year, so a fire first thing in the morning always sounded good. We threw on logs throughout the day, and by dusk, the house was warm and snug and the coals burned crimson while we read our books. I often made my favorite minestrone, especially if I could find good escarole in the market. Or I made my sister-in-law Janet's beautiful chicken soup piled with vegetables, the secret being, as she says, "to not cook them to death."

The soups took on new importance as the forecast turned to snow. Biagio and Angela warned us that the streets shut down when it does snow, and the town's snow plows may or may not come for a day or two, so we should be prepared. I stashed two or three soups and some bread in the freezer and waited with more than a little shiver of anticipation. Living in metropoles like New York and San Francisco for most of my life, the idea that you needed to be prepared to be on your own for days on end was new for me. Sure, I had lived through short power outages or even earthquakes that could disrupt creature comforts. But living out in the country, perhaps cut off from basic services, day in and day out, was a new reality for me to grasp. Then one afternoon the sky turned a deep, flat gray. The wind stopped. And slowly, gently, flakes began to fall. On the grass. On the pool. On our terra-cotta terrace and on our roof tiles. All afternoon the snow continued, softly, but incessantly. It continued through the night, and all the next day. It finally stopped in the middle of the second night, but by the time I woke up, over three feet of snow had fallen. Outside, there was nothing but pure, white, crystalline snow as far as I could see. There was not a sound, nothing, and aside from my own crunching footsteps, there was only a hush. Suddenly I heard the chatter of birds, and as I walked across the terrace and peered around the corner, I saw our persimmon tree. It was still loaded with maybe a hundred bright orange globes of fruit, but now each was topped with a dollop of snow, like a hundred frosted cupcakes, with dozens of hungry birds happily feeding on them like children at a birthday party. As I walked back in the house, I heard the sound of an approaching tractor. It was Biagio's son, Davide, here to plow our driveway for us, with Biagio following behind him with a shovel. All I could do to thank them in return was to offer them a tin of my sister-in-law's chicken soup. It was not enough. I can never seem to thank them enough, but it was something.

As Christmas drew near, Kim became increasingly obsessed with the Feast of the Seven Fishes. He insisted he read somewhere, and he cannot remember where, about something called the Feast of the Seven Fishes and that it is what Italians eat on Christmas Eve. I have heard from Italian American friends that on Christmas Eve they would serve a dinner with several courses, all fish, since it is a holy day of obligation for Catholics, and traditionally that means only fish. But in Italy, the Feast of the Seven Fishes is not a thing. No one I talk to here has heard about it, either. I Google it and find nothing. This does not stop Kim from constantly planning which seven fishes we will be serving on Christmas Eve. On Christmas Eve there will be two people for dinner. My husband. And me. I like fish, but am a little cautious about shellfish, unless they are very familiar to me, like the shrimp or the Dungeness crab we enjoyed in

San Francisco. My husband, by stark contrast, can eat bouillabaisse, cioppino, paella, or any other kind of random fish stew at any time, and in any country, and be thrilled. I like my fish simple. But as Christmas neared, I gave up protesting. His mind was made up.

Ever since we moved here, we had been looking for a really great fishmonger, and we finally found one that fall, in a little tucked-away corner of Alba, half an hour's drive away. It is a family business, called Pescheria del Molo, and it is run by a troop of weathered, boisterous men, one blue-eyed boy about nineteen, and one lovely, patient woman. Every time we go there it is an adventure. The young man speaks some English, so when we walk in, he takes over. The older men tease him, and cuff him lightly on the head when I compliment his English. He blushes.

The first time we walked in, they had swordfish. One enormous whole swordfish, strung up from the ceiling by his long, pointed bill, with his three-foot-long torso laid out along the counter. They sliced it from tail to head, one steak at a time, as customers ordered it, which we also did. The fish hung there with his mouth wide open, and that startled look of the truly freshest fish. The flesh was firm and pale pink, with only the very slightest scent of pure ocean. It was a sight to behold and even better to eat, grilled with piles of sliced lemon and olive oil.

Shortly before Christmas, we drove to Molo to preorder our seven fish, with plans to pick them up on Christmas Eve. Of course, we ordered swordfish. They also always have beautiful Norwegian salmon, which I love, and so we ordered a portion of it. That made two out of seven. My husband then took over, and decided he would make *baccalà*, which is dried cod that has been cured with salt. He had ordered it for lunch one day in Venice and proclaimed it to be amazing. I was not at all sure about baccalà, so I told him he was on his own. I would be fine with the swordfish and salmon, which was already twice as much as I needed for a nice Christmas Eve dinner. Anyway, he was now at three of seven. We could agree on shrimp, and I would eat one. He then ordered a dozen oysters and a little squid, none of which I would eat. But he was still only at six. The Feast of the Six Fishes would not do, no matter how much I lobbied for it. But then we spied a single lobster, a lone Maine lobster, splayed out over the ice. It looked so familiar and comforting and Christmassy, we decided that was it. That made seven. And we were set. My husband was thrilled. I was worried. I could just imagine how I might feel on Christmas morning after a rich dinner of various and assorted seafoods. So we agreed: I would have one small piece of salmon and swordfish, along with one shrimp. And a green salad. He would take all of the other ingredients, except for the *baccalà*, which he planned to serve as his appetizer, and place them in a big pot with water, wine, garlic, and spices to complete his Feast of the Seven Fishes, three of which were for me. That would be our Christmas Eve dinner. Just the two of us. And seven fish.

As Christmas nears, Piemonte and the Langhe quiet down, and the days feel sacred and understated. There are no noisy ads announcing how many shopping days remain, ads that have always somehow made me feel guilty for either not being finished with my shopping weeks in advance or for not making enough appropriately decorated cookies. Here, I did not see many wreaths, Santas, or decorations, either, other than some festive lights stretched out gaily on the roofs and balconies of homes and shops. And there are few Christmas trees. In fact, it was nearly impossible to find a living tree for our home, not an artificial one, but I was determined. We visited three different towns before we finally found the very last, real, scrawny, slightly off-center tree at a nursery twenty-five minutes away. I was delighted. We stuffed it in our trunk and brought it home, set it on a small table in the living room in front of one of the old stone walls, and strung it with colored lights.

Next, I dug out all of my mother's white Lladro porcelain Christmas bells that no one else in the family would take, dozens of them, and hung them carefully on the spiky limbs with thin red satin ribbons. As I held up each one, heavier than they looked, and quite lovely, really, I thought of my mother. She had gleefully ordered one or two for herself every Christmas, and then began gifting them to me and to my brother's wives, blissfully unaware that none of us wanted them. It is funny, but when she died, I realized I not only wanted them, I needed them. Every last one. Not surprisingly, my sisters-in-law were glad to donate their stash to me. And as I looked at the display of bells on the branches, graceful, a little old-fashioned, yet awfully dear, I knew my mom was still with me, here in Italy, at Christmas. We topped the little tree with a giant angel that Kim had in his family years ago. In the evening, lit and cheerful, it was as lovely a tree as I can remember having.

Around noon on Christmas Eve, we drove back to Alba and Pescheria del Molo to pick up the fish we had ordered. The men and the young man, and even the lovely woman, seemed delighted to see us, and heartily wished us a *Buon Natale*. I handed them our credit card, and taking our two sacks from them, glanced at the receipt; we paid nearly one hundred euros for fish for two people. How could that be? We looked at the receipt again. It was clear. It cost fifteen euros for all the fish and shellfish, and eighty-two for the lobster. No wonder they were so happy to see us. Kim and I walked to the car, laughing at what foreigners we still were, and noting we have so much to learn. Next year, we will skip the Maine lobster.

That evening, in our living room, we sat by a crackling fire, with but two presents under our cheerful tree, one for each of us. We popped a bottle of champagne and toasted first to our family, who we were missing, but also to the incredible year we had experienced thus far. Then we sat down to a candlelit dinner of the Feast of the Seven/Three Fishes, a loaf of my husband's sourdough bread, and, of course, more champagne. As I climbed the stairs that night to my bed, in my home in Italy, I could hear the words my father said to me every Christmas Eve, tucking me in and opening my curtains a bit, in case I wanted to check for Santa: "Remember, tonight is a magic night."

The next morning, after opening our two presents, Kim startled me by suggesting that we attend Mass in the old church in Monforte, Madonna della Neve, Our Lady of the Snow. A proclaimed agnostic, he had never suggested going to church with me before. But the idea of getting a little dressed up, going into town, seeing our neighbors, and acknowledging the holiday sounded wonderful to both of us. I thought a prayer or two couldn't hurt, as well.

In our Sunday best, we chose a pew at the back of the church, among the ones that are labeled *uomini*. These are the rows designated for the men in the congregation, maybe so the ladies do not need to try and peer over men's heads to see the priest, or maybe just so the men can sneak out early for a cigarette and an espresso. Or both. Either way, it made me more comfortable to leave the front of the church to those who knew what they were doing throughout the Mass. The church was surprisingly full, especially since the town itself had been so quiet these past few weeks. The altar was laden with evergreens and poinsettias and sprawling white flowers. All of the ten crystal chandeliers that hang from the ceiling were brightly lit, and the beautiful teal and gold frescoes on the ceiling were on full display, the striped pillars throughout the church draped with festive greens. The steady voice of the pastor, the very same one who had blessed our home that summer, was calming. I was surprised to note that he used the informal *tu* as he called on God to help us sinners through our new year ahead, and I remembered just enough from the English Mass to confirm a few Italian words I thought I recognized. At once familiar and foreign, it was deeply comforting.

After Mass, we decided to walk over to Grappolo D'Oro in the piazza for a coffee, and were delighted to find there nearly every one of the people we knew in town, all drinking Bellinis. All of the Rinaldis and their staff, of course; all of the young ladies from Pizza in the Piazza; Silvia and most of her crew; and even some of the folks from the bakery, bank, and the pharmacy. Alberto and Pierre Paolo offered a Bellini to us as well, and we toasted our neighbors with *Tanti Auguri! Buon Natale*, and Merry Christmas all around.

We felt honored to be the only Americans in the piazza that morning, and to be given another little window into life in this most beautiful of towns. It was yet another gift among the many we had received that year.

✺✺✺The Feast of the Seven Fishes✺✺✺

*NOTE: Notwithstanding the delicious and interesting feast Kim created for the two of us on that first Christmas Eve, here is what he would recommend as his ideal Feast of the Seven Fishes, using six types of seafood.

> 2 tablespoons olive oil
> 1 medium onion, chopped
> ½ bulb of fennel, sliced
> 1 green pepper, diced
> 2 cloves garlic, minced
> One 12-ounce can diced tomatoes
> 2 cups water
> 2 cups vegetable stock
> 2 lemons, zested and juiced
> ¼ cup parsley, minced
> 18 saffron threads soaked in hot water for at least an hour
> 2 teaspoons dried oregano
> 2 teaspoons salt
> Fresh ground pepper, to taste
> Cracked red pepper, to taste
> 1 cup little neck clams in their shells, plus 4 ounces white wine
> ½ pound of fresh cod, and ½ pound fresh halibut
> 12 ounces large shrimp, cleaned and peeled with tails on
> 1 cup of oysters and their juice
> 6 ounces cooked Dungeness crab meat
> More chopped parsley and lemon wedges for garnishing

In a giant pot, heat olive oil over moderate heat. Add the onion, fennel, and green pepper. Sauté the vegetables until the onion is translucent and the fennel and green pepper are soft. Add the garlic and sauté for just a minute, but do not let it brown. Add tomatoes, water, vegetable stock, the lemon juice and zest, and stir. Add parsley, saffron threads in their soaking water, oregano, salt, pepper, and some cracked red pepper. (Reserve a little cracked red pepper to add at the end if more kick is desired.)

Let the broth simmer for half an hour or so. Just before you are ready to eat, steam the clams separately in the wine and discard any clams that do not open. Then to the giant pot, add the cod and halibut, flaking the fish as it cooks. Add the shrimps until they curl and turn opaque. Add the oysters until their edges curl. Add the crab just to heat it through. And finally add the opened cooked clams and their shells, wine broth and all.

Serve in large bowls garnished with a little more chopped parsley and lemon wedges and, if desired, more cracked red pepper. Ideal with hot, crusty sourdough bread.

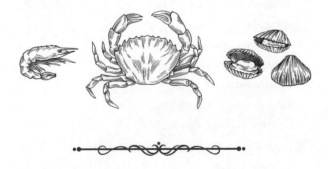

GENNAIO

Winter in the Langhe is very dark and still, with the sun not up until nearly nine in the morning, and setting again by five. It can also be dank and sometimes rainy or snowy, and there is little traffic on the streets. It is the time of year when the businesses in town are shuttered for a month or two, although they seem to alternate closures, with one place always left open for groceries, one for coffee, and one for lunch, dinner, and drinks. I imagine it is all planned out that way in advance. It is a good time for the businesses to do a serious cleaning, and for the owners to take a much-needed respite, maybe a long trip to a sun-drenched beach in Asia or South America. I think Italians appreciate the importance of time off, better than we Americans do. For those of us still here, it makes for a very empty town center. Yet I was steadfast in my desire to experience the entire year here, at least once, if only to feel the fullness of each of the seasons throughout the region.

Actually, I like it quiet. The people we do encounter in the piazza are happy to see us, and have time to chat. Silvia invites live musicians to play at her Barolo Bar every Wednesday evening, so it is always full, lively, and warm even on the snowiest of nights. During the day, I have time for long walks, and long hours trying to unlock the Rubik's Cube of Italian grammar. In all, it proved to be a good time for becoming more familiar with our community, and the crisp, cold air, and oaky fires really were beautiful in their own right.

In our little commune of Roddino, many businesses close as well. Early in January, we had dinner at La Torricella, the restaurant and inn closest to our home. As Francesco was clearing our table, we asked if they, too, had plans for closing. He said that they would close for two months, but the first few weeks of closure are always spent working around the albergo and readying things for the upcoming season, before he and his family head out to Spain for a vacation in the sun.

"What kinds of things do you do to get ready for the upcoming season?" asked my ever curious husband.

Francesco spoke enough English to answer, "First we make salami." He continued, "*Tutti noi*, all of us, come and we make our salami. *E dopo*, after, we hang it up in the barn until spring. The salami you are eating tonight is what we made last year."

My husband thought about this for a minute and then asked, "Can I help?"

Francesco paused, taken aback at first, and then graciously said, "*Certo*. Why not?" And the plan was made. My husband was expected at eight thirty in the morning on the following Monday at the back of the kitchen. There would be coffee.

Kim, excited but a touch apprehensive, arrived promptly at eight thirty, greeted by the ever smiling Francesco; his wife and chef, the lovely Alessandra; her sister who is also the winemaker; their brother; their parents; two family friends; and two of the staff waiters, who were all already deep into the task at hand. Stacked on the floor were giant plastic tubs filled with five hundred pounds of pork shoulder in chunks somewhat bigger than a football. There were massive vats of wine simmering on the stove emitting heady aromas, especially for that hour of the day. There was a large work table where Alessandra and her sister, with their impressive knife skills, spread out the meat like dead animals and masterfully trimmed it of fat and grizzle. Kim, who had no particularly masterful knife skills, was given a job even he could handle. He was asked to simply take the perfectly trimmed pork and cut it into pieces small enough to fit into a meat grinder. The father, Diego, ground the meat until he had filled a large tub two-thirds full, then ground a twenty-pound slab of lard, pure white pork fat, and piled it on top of the pork. Next, the two family friends spent hours bent over the vat, mixing up all the meat and lard gently by hand, lubricating it along with various quantities of the warm red wine until the lard was properly dispersed throughout the meat.

But the true magic occurred when the sister and father huddled off in the corner, carefully measuring out their mysterious blend of salts and spices in secret amounts. It was when they added this special mixture to the meat and lard that the transformation from raw meat to salami began. It was at that point that Francesco appeared with his usual smile and a spoon, scooped up a chunk of the raw salami mixture, and took a big bite. He looked up at my husband, and as if to challenge him, offered him a spoon as well. What could Kim do but match him, bite for bite? Afterward, Kim admitted to me that the *salame crudo* was delicious. Strange, but delicious. Although, he also said the real highlight of that first day was the hearty and convivial lunch served to all, even the children, in the back of the restaurant's kitchen.

The next day, the group returned to funnel the meat mixture into miles of intestines, forming them into sausages. My husband was given the only job that required no skill or prior experience. They handed him what looked like two hairbrushes, but were actually lethal wooden tools studded with sharp, pointy spikes. He was to poke holes into the newly formed sausages to fully aerate the meat, allowing it to cure. For the entire day he went up and down the yards and yards of links, pounding them, poking hole after hole. He said he found the task pleasingly mindless. Then, finally, when all the salami was stuffed, he was allowed to help the men carry the three hundred kilos of links into the shed, where they would hang for months until they emerged, aged into La Torricella's signature salami.

On the afternoon of the second day, Alessandra prepared a celebratory lunch that was really a modest feast. The entire group of salami makers sat around a beautifully laden table in the restaurant's atrium and shared platters of *tajarin* and ragu, roasted veal with vegetables, salad, bread, and a hazelnut torte.

I admit it. I was jealous. I would have loved to have experienced such an intimate, authentic, and vital part of our local culture. But I was also emboldened by my husband's success. I made up my mind that I would somehow find a way to realize my culinary dream of witnessing the weekly making of plin, at Roddino's renowned Osteria Da Gemma. And one day soon afterwards, I did.

FEBBRAIO

I have said before that, in fact, life here is not perfect. Yes, it is beautiful, relaxing, and a continual feast for the senses. But, in addition to the annual invasion of ants, which I am still just getting over, the erratic internet, and the ugly business with our real estate agent Mario, there is another frustration. In Italy, things can be just the teensiest bit bureaucratic. Okay, it can be more than a teensy bit. Getting things done can be incredibly, painstakingly slow, like the aging of a fine Barolo, the ripening of a good Parmesan, or the putting of a man on the moon. A case in point is the saga of my car's license plates.

We had shipped my 2007 Lexus from San Francisco to Italy in December just before we moved here. Why not? It still had a few good years on it, we loved the car, and it only cost a few thousand dollars to ship it. However, once it disappeared into the moving van in front of our apartment, it fell off the radar screen. For two months, all we received were vague missives about its whereabouts. No one person seemed responsible for it. The shippers were not only unsure when it would arrive; they were not exactly sure where it was. I began to panic. Finally, in May, we received word that our Lexus would be arriving in Livorno, after having been lost for months somewhere in Korea. I am not the best geography student, but I am pretty sure Korea is not on the way to Europe, no matter how you do the math. And on that hot afternoon when the car finally did show up in the gigantic parking lot at Livorno's port, I found that my battery had been switched out for a completely dead one, and the license plates had been stolen. Why would anyone want my California license plates? I could picture them hanging on the wall of a dorm room in Seoul.

Fortunately, I had taken a taxi to the port, and the driver was as considerate as all of the Italians I have met here in Piemonte. He helped me jump-start the car, then he told me to follow him to a reliable auto mechanic where I bought a new battery. And then the taxi driver found a piece of white paper and a felt pen, and proceeded to create a new license plate for me using my old California numbers. It looked ridiculous, of course, but at least I was able to drive the car all the way back to Monforte, which was a huge relief.

Then we began the unbelievable process of registering the car in Italy. The first step was to become a legal resident. Even before moving here, we filled a three-inch binder of documents for the Italian consulate in San Francisco (tax returns, fingerprints, letters from several bankers, and photos in triplicate, etc., etc.). It turns out that was nothing compared to what Italy now wanted from us. We lost track after counting twenty-two different visits to different towns, different bureaus, and different police stations. We then had to travel to Alba to take a two-day course on the laws, customs, and practices in Italy. We needed to try and learn Italian (we were getting better, but it was still a work in progress, to be sure). One year and dozens of appointments later, my husband and I became proud, card-carrying Italian residents.

But that was merely Step One. Step Two began with the search for a place where we could obtain actual license plates. We spent three days browsing Google, and made three more trips to Alba. One motor vehicle club, two car dealers, and one vague "agency" later, we were given a comprehensive list of what was required to register the car. In addition to our residency cards, we needed the original title, drivers' licenses, and various forms and letters, all notarized. That required actually flying back to the United States and driving to the state capital in Sacramento to obtain a special document that said the notary in Sacramento was legitimate. Of course, the Sacramento notary used the wrong form the first time so we had to do this twice.

Meanwhile, all this time, we had been driving around Italy in a car with handmade paper plates. We were stopped by the police twice, once in Turin and once at the French border, and both times it required painfully long explanations in various languages about who the hell we were, and why we have had hand-scribbled plates for the past year. But both times we escaped jail. And, blessedly, most police seemed to give our car a second look, then think better of it, as if imagining the amount of painful red tape they would need to go through if they actually hauled us in.

The next several steps were even more complicated and frustrating, involving Lexus of Manhattan, Lexus headquarters in Los Angeles, and various dealerships, agencies, and motor vehicle bureaus in Italy. I will spare you the details because, as they say, if I told you everything, I would have to kill you. But suffice it to say, we went through several thousands of dollars, dozens of emails (thank God for Google Translate), hours on the phone in my elementary Italian, and at least a few bottles of Arneis before we found an official who was as tired of this process as we were, took pity on two immigrants from San Francisco, and finally said, "*Sì*."

When we placed our brand-spanking-new license plate on our old car, it looked remarkably similar to the paper one, but with fewer wrinkles. In retrospect, we didn't really suffer from the waiting, much. And now, fifteen months later, it is done. I smile every time I see it. And the letters are ZA (short for pizza, my favorite food) and EC (short for the new European Community where I live) so it is the first license plate I have ever had that I can always remember.

Like the Slow Food movement that started here, life is slower. But it is still pretty darn sweet.

Photos
A year in Piemonte

CHAPTER THIRTEEN

Taking apart an old house and putting it back together again changes you in a way I would have never anticipated. It becomes a part of you, and eventually, you a part of it. Whenever I lay on the couch and stare at the soaring walls, the layers of years written into the stones, I think of the people who carried these rocks and pointed these bricks.

I found myself becoming more and more curious about and connected to the woman who was born in the house, and who died in it some ninety-five years later, just before we made it ours. I learned from Angela and Biagio that her name was Emma. But who was she? What was she like? I was touched, even a little embarrassed, at the intimacy of entering her bedroom for the first time with the crucifix she left on the wall and the pink beaded rosary I found in the drawer beside her bed. I kept the rosary and her neatly framed prints of the Blessed Virgin and Pope John. And Angela brought me some weathered, sepia photos of Emma and her brother proudly posing in front of our house, showing off their new tractor and motorcycle probably sometime in the 1940s. I was particularly curious to learn from Biagio that Emma never married, and lived alone in the big house, until her later years when she cared for her brother here after his wife passed away. But what defined Emma? Did she love the view of Monviso covered in snow against a crystal blue sky on a winter's day? Was she, too, startled at how very early the birds' insistent singing announced the sunrise in June? Did she smile at the crazy sound of barking deer that call to one another in the valleys at dusk? Was she ever in love, and did she lose her life's love during the war? Did she sometimes suffer hunger, or was her vegetable garden enough to see her through the war and other hard times? Did she fight in the war, brandish a gun, or maybe secretly help the Partisans struggle in the Resistance?

Down in our cantina, carved into the very back of the wine cellar, is a small arched doorway leading to a tunnel that feeds out to the gully behind the house. It is so small that I would need to crouch to enter, and Kim would need to almost crawl, not that I could ever summon the courage to try. But I often wondered if this was for the residents to flee the Nazis, or if it was simply a shortcut to the valley out back. Some people here say that our cantina housed the Partisans and their meetings, so maybe this was their escape route. Or maybe it had a more pragmatic function, like a shortcut for shuttling hay into the barn from the fields, or for losers at poker to ditch out of the game at night quickly. And outside our kitchen door is a brick and stone building that used to serve as the neighborhood forno where families would take turns coming to bake their bread. I try to picture the convivial scene of neighbors arriving, sharing an espresso and some local gossip, and wish we could start that tradition here again, firing up the giant oven and having everyone over while their bread and focaccia are being baked.

Still, as old as this house is, there is nothing ghostly about these rooms. They feel like ours now, beautiful in their own way and very much alive in this decade, however weathered and out of scale they might be. I do sometimes wonder what Emma would have thought of us, living in her house, and in her barn. Americans, reworking her house so dramatically and even putting in something as frivolous as a swimming pool—what would she have thought? Oh, and what tales Emma could have told me.

To think that now we have become a part of this storied home. We are another layer of people who have made their mark, for better or worse, on this three-hundred-year-old structure, in this centuries-old town. We are a part of it all.

Angela has told me that her family is happy to have our house living again. Here in Italy, she said, there are living homes, and those that have been abandoned for generations and are crumbling away. Ours was living. Zef told me he believed our home has an *anima*, a soul he could feel sometimes when he was working alone in the house, while he was bringing it back from disrepair. I feel it, too. But it feels anything but ghoulish.

Spring returned to the Langhe, chilly and wet at times, but fresh and green and dotted with bright pops of flowers throughout the hillsides. We were finally realizing our shared dream, learning a new language, a new cuisine, and living more slowly, breathing a little more deeply. We were surrounded by beauty, in the landscape and in the people we were getting to know. Sometimes, I could feel flashes of oddly familiar sensations from my childhood here—the scent of a smoky wood fire or newly mown grass, the tingle of a sunburned belly, a birdsong—awakening senses reminiscent of an innocence, a simplicity, a saner way of being. Nothing had driven us to this; it just seemed to have come to us. Like love. And now it was a part of us, who we were, what our home was.

One night lying in bed, unable to sleep, I said, "Kim?"

"Yes?"

"I am not ready to go back to live in San Francisco." There was a long pause in the dark. I heard the steady beating of rain on the roof and the gurgling of the drain pipe.

Then he said, "I've had the same thought." He rolled over. "But our tenants are moving out at the end of the month. The tax implications of that would be enormous. If we decide to stay in Italy, we would need to sell the apartment in San Francisco, and sell it now."

There was another long pause. I took a deep breath. "I am okay with that," I finally said, only a little bit hesitantly. "I am just not finished with Italy."

"I know what you mean," Kim said with a sigh. "Let's talk about it in the morning." He reached out and squeezed my hand, and we both fell asleep.

In April we flew back to California. Our minds were made up. We would sell our home in San Francisco and make Italy our home. From this point on, there was no looking back.

I called my dear and trusted childhood friend Patti who was a Realtor in San Francisco. The market was good, she assured me, and she encouraged us to list the apartment for more than we could have hoped for. We stayed in a hotel down the peninsula near Kim's mom, and spent time with her and with friends. Of course, it was lovely to see everyone and to be back in California, but I had no misgivings about our decision.

Patti called us the day after our home went on the market. We had three offers already, so we accepted the one that would close most quickly. Patti asked us to come up to San Francisco and sign a large stack of documents, then explained that she could take care of the actual closing from there on out. And that was it. Suddenly we had no home in America. I felt a little bit as if the floor were dropping out from beneath my feet, like in that centrifugal carnival ride, but I also had a sweeping sense of freedom. Now we could focus our energies on Italy. We would continue to visit once or twice a year to see Kim's mother, our kids, our siblings, and their families.

And on this visit, we lingered a little longer than usual, spending a little extra time enjoying family and friends. We took care of routine doctor and dentist appointments, met with our accountant and filed our taxes, doing all the pedestrian tasks that were best done while physically in the States.

Two weeks later, we boarded the plane that would take us back to Italy and our life in the Langhe. For once, I actually slept for a few hours, a peaceful, comforting sleep. As we flew over Switzerland and Northern Italy toward Milan, I slid up the window shade and watched it dawn pink over the massive snowcapped Alps, and felt I was coming home.

By now, we could look forward with eager anticipation as to what we might expect in the year ahead. Spring is such an invigorating time in Roddino and Monforte. The restaurants open again but none of the European tourists have arrived yet, so that we practically have the little towns to ourselves. The flowers are a delight, showy tulips and daffodils sprouting up here and there in everyone's yards. In between the rainy times, there is also plenty of sun, and the days lengthen noticeably one after the other. We spent our time readying the yard for summer, opening the pool, and planting the petunias on the balconies, the kind that drape way down over the side and last all season long. We filled in our new landscaping with more rosemary and lavender, and tried to coax the scrawny little trees in the backyard with daily water and extra fertilizer.

Easter was barely a week away. We awaited the celebrations and the delicious panettone from the bakery in Monforte, *la colomba.* Shaped like a dove for, I suppose, the Holy Spirit, it has a sweet, brioche-like cake on the bottom, then a lighter, almost meringue-type layer on top, all sprinkled with chunky little sugar crystals and laced with almonds, plump raisins, and a dousing of brandy. Unlike the deadly heavy and dry panettones that I have tried from grocery stores or in airport cafes, it is moist, tender, absolutely delicious, and surprisingly addictive. By now we had learned to buy two. One for Easter morning and one to eat in the car on the way home from the bakery.

Zef and his men finished our outdoor patio, *la tettoia*, and we strung up cheerful little white lights, found lanterns and a long table, and looked forward to warm weather. This happened just as we got word that Kim's brother Steve had been successful in convincing their other brother and his wife, plus all of their cousins from Iowa, to come to the Langhe to see us for a reunion in September. It was exciting to have something so grand to plan. I could already imagine the party we would have here to welcome them. *La tettoia* would be the perfect place for us all to dine al fresco.

Next door, Biagio and Angela were hard at work on their *orto*, planting enough vegetables to feed the entire *commune*, and row upon row of tomatoes, salad greens, and cucumbers. It was necessary, they explained happily, because their daughter Manuela and her family would be coming in August from their home in Wisconsin to can their tomatoes for the winter. There was great excitement in the air between our two homes.

Like last year, when the weather turned a bit warmer, Piero and Innes arrived next door from Turin, and even before they unloaded all their bags and boxes, began planting their *orto*. Theirs was a little smaller than Biagio and Angela's, but impeccable. Innes plants flowers each year, and her wisteria annually provides a beautiful cool shade for them to rest in between bouts of digging and raking. Meanwhile, Piero creates magic in the rest of the garden with his rows and rows of vegetables. I can see why some might think it is odd for neighbors to live in such close proximity, literally attached to one another's homes. But we have discovered that our home, our little *borgo*, is nicer because of them. Inevitably we are the benefactors of their gardening skills, with tomatoes that taste like tomatoes, green and yellow beans still warm from the sun, and zucchini with flowers still attached offered to us almost weekly. And our days are more interesting, our conversations more lively when they are there.

One warm evening, sitting by our pool, Piero joined us, as Innes was not feeling well. The water was still too cold for him to swim, but he seemed to relish the sun and the company, as did we. My husband poured each of us a glass of Nebbiolo. Then Piero began to talk about the days when Emma lived in the house we now occupied, and I took the opportunity to do some digging. *"Parlami di Emma,"* I said to him. Tell me about her. What was she like?

He leaned back in his chair, and began to reminisce. Emma was *"una meraviglia,"* he recalled, a marvel. Quiet. Strong. Very capable. She stayed single her whole life, never married. I asked why he thought she never found someone, and he had no idea. She was somewhat older than he was, and would have never confided in him. But he knew she took good care of her brother, and that said a lot to him about her character. A single woman of her generation would need to be pretty secure, pretty independent to not have a husband. He remembered that she had a cow, a few goats and sheep that she kept right where we built our living room. And she made wonderful Toma cheese, in her little kitchen, where our front door is now. It gave me such joy to think of Toma being made here in this house where I live. I asked Piero if Emma was a Partisan, and he said yes, definitely. Her mother and her whole family were very supportive of the Italian Resistance, and they used to tell stories about how they would hide Partisan soldiers under the hay in their hayloft when the enemy came around. That is exactly where we were sleeping now, I realized, and the thought gave me a chill. But it also gave me comfort to realize that Emma was loved, if only by her family and neighbors. I can see where that could be enough.

At the end of June, we traveled back to the States for the very best of reasons: Flynn and Katherine's wedding. It was as beautiful, youthful, and joyful as they were. The ceremony was held in a grassy meadow, set against the backdrop of Sun Valley's craggy Sawtooth Mountains, contrasted by the wedding party in formal tuxes and white satin and lace, as well as an abundance of family and friends.

I woke up each day that week and practically sprinted through the day, from event to event, filled with much laughter and a few tears, trying to take it all in. Kim and I hosted the rehearsal dinner, which was an honor. In lieu of a long speech, Kim and I, along with the rest of the wedding party, managed to pull off an a cappella flash mob performance of Bob Dylan's "Forever Young," although none of us are particularly good singers. Flynn and Katherine were as stunned as they were touched. Cooper and Allie's little son was the triumphant ringbearer, with a gentle assist from Allie, and Kelly was perfectly charming as the best man. And in what was one of the great highlights of my life, tall, handsome Cooper gallantly walked me down the aisle to my seat in the first row. It's hard to be with these young men and women for any length of time without laughing, and I loved every minute of it. For our wedding present and their honeymoon, we sent the newlyweds to our home in the Langhe for one week without us, then we joined them for another week at the end of their visit. The amount of champagne I consumed that month was enough to last me a lifetime.

Once back in Italy, and throughout the time we spent there with our son and radiant new daughter-in-law, I felt relentlessly tired. The festivities, the emotions, and the jet lag took more out of me than it ever had. I took a little longer naps, and tried to find some quiet time for myself when I could. I longed for the days when I used to drink coffee, and could have simply devoured a couple of cups to get my energy back. Instead, I just allowed myself to kick back and relax in the warmth of the summer sun. All in all, lethargy is not a bad way to spend a warm summer, especially when it is a summer in Italy.

August brought with it Manuela, her American husband, Christopher, and their nine-year-old daughter. Manuela was as quick, funny, independent, and charming as her mother, with her father's twinkle. She, her husband, and their coltish young daughter together sent summertime sounds across the yard—of bouncing balls, squeals in the sprinkler, splashing in the pool—that changed the character of our little community, making it feel measurably livelier, happier. But perhaps the best thing about their visit, from my perspective, was that Manuela, who speaks English as well as I do, could finally translate for me so many of the subtle and complicated thoughts I have wanted to communicate to Angela and Biagio these past few years. I could finally express how much we took to heart their friendship, their many kindnesses, and what they have done for us to make this feel like home. They merely blushed at the sentiments, but it made me feel better to finally say it, even if it was in English.

We spent much of the rest of the summer getting ready for our own family's arrival in September. Our cousins would be staying up in Monforte at a villa in the old town, but we were the hosts and, as such, we wanted to plan plenty of activities and outings for them to choose from. We had a welcome dinner in our cantina and organized bike rides and wine tastings. My sister-in-law, Carmen, played tour guide for all on a day trip to Turin. We took a group cooking lesson in the renowned restaurant Guido, where I served as a translator for the chef (secure in the thought that if I made mistakes in the translation, no one would know). We all made *ravioli del plin* and enjoyed the fruits of our labor as part of a superb lunch. There were fancy dinners out, and dinners at our home, supplemented with some of Nicoletta's *plin*. The cousins even cooked for us one night at their lodging. I was so delighted to show them "our" Monforte and Roddino, "our" Langhe, and they were keen participants in it all. By the end of the week, the sun was beginning to set a little earlier and the air reminded us that autumn was near. But cousin Charlie insisted on ending each day with a bone-chilling swim in the unheated pool. He said it made him feel alive. There is nothing more I could ask of a guest than to embrace life that way.

By the time they left in September, I was still tired. Kim joked with some seriousness that we needed a vacation to recover from our vacation. Not needing much encouragement, Rob and Carolyn agreed to fly over and meet us in Sicily, a place none of us had ever visited. The plan was that, afterward, they would fly back up with us to Roddino so we could all put up our feet and enjoy the last days of summer at our home. It sounded perfect to me and it was a welcomed getaway for all of us. But before we left, on the side of caution, I made a doctor's appointment in nearby Alba, a substantial city of over twenty-five thousand residents, to see if there was some explanation for my persistent fatigue. I met with a doctor who performed a few tests and was very reassuring. She said I seemed fine, especially since I had just seen my doctors in San Francisco a few months earlier. We scheduled one last procedure, but she was fully confident that after a restful week in Sicily, my energy would be back to normal. It was a relief.

I love the short trips we can take around Italy and neighboring countries. We arrive, of course, without the jet lag we would have if traveling from America. And we get to explore such a rich palette of places. Sicily is indeed one of those.

Steeped in sun and a colorful if complicated history, Sicily is both educational and indulgent, cultured and wild. I shopped for clothes, which I almost never do, and bought a brightly patterned silk blouse for myself. We strolled through the Teatro Antico di Taormina, Greco-Roman theater ruins. Kim gave me a set of hand-painted Italian ceramic dishes for my birthday, featuring brightly colored lemons to remind me of Sicily. And Rob and Carolyn surprised me with an elegant ceramic platter and a lovely urn adorned with more lemons. I plan to someday bequeath the beautiful pottery to my granddaughter, Cooper and Allie's little girl, whose nickname is, yes, Lemon.

We sat on a sandy white beach in a covered hut where waiters brought us syrupy sweet iced Limoncello. One starlit night we wandered up to a church perched on the hill behind us, surrounded by terraces and wide-open windows, to hear a concert of singers performing arias from well-known Italian operas, and although they were not well known to me, I loved every note. To be out of our routine, but in a country that was becoming so familiar, was wonderful. It makes living in the Langhe so much the lovelier, to be able to take long weekends in other magical places.

Our vacation from our vacation with our friends was a lovely way to end the summer. But I found I now wanted nothing more than to go home to my home, with my husband and friends, fall into a deep slumber in my own bed, awaken to drink my tea, and relax late into the morning, then grill outside every evening and watch the autumn colors start to turn.

Photos Befores and afters

CHAPTER FOURTEEN

It was on the jetway to the plane leaving Sicily that I received a text from my doctor in Italy telling me that I had breast cancer. She said she was sorry but that the tiny lump she had been so certain was benign two weeks earlier was actually malignant. I took my seat, fastened my seat belt, put my tray table and seat back in the full upright position, closed my eyes, and felt the weight of gravity as the earth fell away and the plane lifted into the air.

It is odd when all of your worst fears become real. It is not so bad. Nothing hurt. Nothing felt different. But I knew that it all suddenly was very different, so I settled in and tried to untangle the rush of my thoughts. Kim took my hand, and I felt the warm release of tears. Then I took a deep breath and barely cried again for the rest of the long year ahead. I didn't have time. I needed all of my energy, every breath, every thought, every drop of positivity I could muster to get me well. This is not to say that I didn't feel sorry for myself from time to time or experience rolling waves of fear. There would be days that I could not wait to end so that I could cross them off the calendar and move on to the next one. But on that day and each of the days that followed, I did my best to manage hour by hour, until the day passed.

Together, my husband and I decided that I should be treated in the United States. We would need to go back to San Francisco, where we had our doctors and friends to support us. And since we no longer had a home there, we would rent a place for as long as was necessary and return to Italy when we could. We agreed we should leave as soon as possible.

What my husband did not know at that moment was that our three sons, their wives, and I had been planning for them to all travel to our home in Italy to surprise him on his seventieth birthday, which was five weeks away. This surprise was going to be my present to him. We had not all been under the same roof at the same time in over five years, and after all, we had designed the layout of our home in Italy specifically to allow all of us to spend time here together. Still, I needed to find out if waiting yet another several weeks for surgery and treatment would put me at risk.

I devoted a week or two to furtive phone calls in the middle of the night with doctors and nurses in California. I learned that while my tumor was small, my type of breast cancer, called Triple Negative, was the kind most likely to return and was particularly aggressive. This was not the news I wanted to hear. And for a while, the only additional news I received was bad news.

Finally, one particularly thoughtful nurse practitioner told me that while my diagnosis was not ideal, breast cancer is not an emergency. She advised that a once-in-a-lifetime event like the surprise we were planning for my husband's birthday would be a risk I should consider taking. When I spoke about it with my lovely daughter-in-law Allie, she said, "If you need to come back home, we will understand. But as far as we are concerned, we are coming to Italy!" That convinced me. I set an appointment at UCSF for five days after my husband's birthday and put my fate in God's loving hands.

Rob and Carolyn were still with us during those few tumultuous days after Sicily, before they were to go home to California, and we managed to enjoy some great dinners, a few hands of bridge (the kind with real cards), a few glasses of good wine, and some belly laughs, as always. In my conversations with UCSF, it became clear that if I wanted to hit the ground running with my treatment after I returned to San Francisco, the doctors there needed to have the physical slide from my biopsied tumor in their hands, the one that was currently with my doctor in Italy. That is when Carolyn did something I will never forget. She volunteered to fly home to San Diego as planned, hand-carrying my slide in her purse, guarding it with her life, then catch the next plane up to San Francisco and personally deliver my biopsied specimen to UCSF.

That one giant gesture saved me three weeks or more of waiting for my treatment to begin, which meant I could safely stay in Italy for Kim's birthday surprise. I can only imagine how tired and jet-lagged she was afterward, not to mention how she must have filled out her customs declaration. And it is all you need to know about what kind of a person, what kind of a friend, Carolyn is.

On the afternoon of my husband's birthday, a Sunday, he was upstairs in our room, reading, and just possibly napping. He still had no clue that there was any kind of celebration planned for him. I called up to him and asked him to please come downstairs right away. He didn't answer for a minute, so I called again.

He said, "What is it, Barbara?" He never calls me Barbara unless he is not happy. "I am trying to read."

I insisted. "Please come down here. Now. It is important."

I heard him sigh heavily and he opened the bedroom door and lumbered across the way to the edge of the stairs overlooking the living room. Then he stopped, put his hand to his mouth, and began to back away.

"Oh my God! What . . . the . . . ?"

Below, in the living room, were all of our beautiful children, wives, kids, and all, holding glasses of champagne (or apple juice), and looking up at him, toasting him.

Finally, Cooper broke the silence, saying, "Happy Birthday!" and then the cacophony began as off-key strains of "Happy Birthday" filled the house.

My stunned husband, still speechless, stumbled backward a bit until I led him downstairs to the open arms of those seven precious humans. They had flown in from Singapore, Boston, and Boise.

"How did you . . . when did you . . ." No more words came. The next four days were the kind that float by effortlessly, and leave no traces beyond a blur of pure contentment. I kept the video that I took of Kim on my cell phone, so overwhelmed by their faces that he could not find his breath, and it sustained me through every day of my treatment.

CHAPTER FIFTEEN

For the next ten months, I put nearly all thoughts of Monforte and Roddino and the Langhe into the back of my brain. Sometimes at night, though, I would fall into bed, pull the covers up over my head, close my eyes, pretend I was in our Italian home, and slip peacefully into a deep slumber. But mostly I could not think about it. I could conceive of only where I actually was, concentrating on the moment at hand. If I had stopped to also think about what I was missing, the year would have become unbearable.

And then, in time, the months of treatment were but a memory.

By September, with my surgery, chemotherapy, and radiation finished, and my energy ever so slowly returning, I arrived back in Italy. As my husband drove us the two hours from the airport to our little town, I was astonished. The fields were more velvety green, lush, and verdant than I remembered, and the little hill towns and castles even more like from a storybook. Was it always so incredibly beautiful? The undulating road through the vineyards rocked and soothed me, and I felt a warm contentment run through my veins, through my gut, into my soul.

Even before going to our house, we stopped by Trattoria dell'Amicizia to say hello to dear Nicoletta. She ran out from the kitchen and threw her arms around me, smothering both of us. There were more huge hugs for my husband. She then delivered the sad news that she and Fabio had split up and he was now living near Turin. We both looked at each other through our tears and she shrugged. "*Eh, la vita!*" We promised that we would help each other through.

When we pulled into the gravel driveway leading to our house, Piero was standing in his garden and shouted, "*Mamma mia!! Che brava!*" and embraced us both. He looked at me, with no hair and a pink baseball cap, and proclaimed that he thought that, without hair, I was even more beautiful, saying a lot about how kind he is, but not a lot about my hair. Innes appeared at their door and also greeted us with such love and warmth, I could not speak. Then, with a mischievous smile, Piero pulled out a piece of paper that his granddaughter had prepared for him. On it was written, phonetically, so he could read it aloud: "ello kim uelchom bek, nais siin iu." "Hello, Kim. Welcome back. Nice seeing you."

And we were not in the door for more than a minute when Angela and Biagio arrived with an armful of flowers from their garden. They had been watching for our arrival and strode across both of our yards to greet us. I could not look at their shining faces without more tears appearing, although they just smiled as if it were perfectly normal for us to have been gone for ten months and for me to be bald.

It was the best homecoming anyone could have asked for, hands down. I left my suitcase in the kitchen and went straight upstairs to my room, pushing open the shutters to the brilliance of the afternoon. I slipped on my swimsuit and walked out to the backyard, feeling happier than I could remember ever having been before. Floating on my back in the cold pool, I felt the hot Italian sun on my face and took a long, deep, whole breath. I was alive. And I was home.

None of us escape this life unscathed, or unscarred. None of us make the long life journey without heartache or loss. It is not that bad things, hard things, don't happen. They will. What matters, though, is how incredibly the good things calm the sting. What matters is that we set ourselves up to catch the good things in our nets and keep them near. The friendships. The kindnesses. The tulip that bursts through the melting snow to announce the sun. The perfect morsel of food prepared in the simplest way, with care. The love that arrives late, just when any hope of love seems gone. The friendships that spring from nothing but goodwill. And the home that springs from a crumbling, rusted ruin. Sometimes it takes courage to grab the good things when they arrive, and sometimes it just takes luck.

I am lucky. I live in a town that is made of the stuff of fairy tales.

Photos

In the end

⁂ *Aperol Spritz Cocktail* ⁂

Ice
Aperol liqueur
Alta Langa Brut or champagne
Sparkling water
Orange slice

Add ice to a large wineglass until nearly full. Pour in equal parts Aperol and Alta Langa Brut or champagne. Add a splash of sparkling water on top and an orange slice to garnish. Perfect for floating in a pool on a warm summer afternoon.

AFTERWORD

February 2020: The years have been sliding by, one into the other. We spend most of our time in Italy, when we can, alone or with family and friends visiting. I jealously guard some time for just the two of us there, amidst our Italian community, as we are becoming a part of the fabric of it and feeling oddly more at home than we have any right to. Their holidays now feel like our holidays, and the familiar faces of our neighbors make my heart full almost the way our lifelong friends do. This is very much our home.

We leave Italy during the coldest and darkest months to spend the holidays in America with our children as well as our grandchildren, who are growing by inches every time I turn my back, becoming interesting little persons in their own right. We check in with our doctors and we celebrate the good fortune of the great health we enjoy. I have been cancer-free since my surgery and have every intention of staying that way. I love the ease of being back in California where there is always something to entertain us, and always business to attend to. But I truly thrive in Italy.

My husband has planted a small vineyard in our yard in Italy and is growing Barbera grapes, more as an homage to the great wines that grow around us than anything else. He has named it Barbera di Barbara. It is humbling how much work goes into one plant, one bottle of wine; it takes years to have grapes old enough to harvest, and another year or two to be drinkable. If and when we finally do have a bottle of wine to enjoy, it will be to toast the real winemakers around us who have spent generations perfecting their art, and who have so generously shared some of their wisdom with us.

I need to see my oncologists every six months, still. So, we have come to California for the winter, and have made plans for our springtime return. It is essential that my husband be there soon to prune the new little vines, after the final snow of winter, but before warm days ignite their buds' growth. And, of course, I am anxious to return to my home and watch the days lengthen and our gardens spring back to life.

But then I come upon some unsettling news. I hear about a rogue virus that had overtaken a city in China, and then spread to a cruise ship heading for San Francisco. It sounds frightening, yet very far away. Oddly, I read, a few cases of this strange virus have now been reported in Rome and Milan, especially Milan. This is not the lead story on the news, with our elections taking the foreground, but I do hear of it and it catches my attention.

Each passing day brings another mention of this virus. They are calling it the coronavirus, and it seems to be spreading somewhat voraciously through Lombardia, the province neighboring our Piemonte. There are even some deaths reported, an elderly woman aboard a cruise ship and perhaps another in Italy. The news from China is becoming grim, and I fear for a friend of mine, Father Frank, who is visiting mainland China for the Chinese New Year. I message him on social media and urge him to come home, but he shrugs me off, telling me not to worry, he is wearing a mask everywhere and will come home as planned in a week or so.

Like a slow drumbeat, word of this virus in Italy pops into my news feed, day after day. It is beginning to make headlines now. On the first Sunday in March, the *Bloomberg* feed, under their "Politics" section, reads:

Italy Locks Down Rich North as
Conte Tries to Contain Panic

5,883 cases on Saturday with 233 deaths

Even under normal circumstances, news of Italy will catch my ear, and now, suddenly, it is everywhere. My husband and I decide to move our flight to Italy back a month, from March until late April, hoping for some quick resolution of the outbreak. But within a week it becomes clear that this virus is spreading throughout Italy exponentially, especially in our area to the north.

We speak with our Italian friends and learn that all schools and most businesses are shut down, all events canceled, and people are required to stay at home. We have a video chat with Nicoletta who has just boarded up her iconic Trattoria dell'Amicizia. She is laughing and sweet as always, yet tells us she is heartbroken not to be cooking and serving her plin to the workers no longer coming for lunch each day, or her famed veal roasted in Barolo sauce to the couples who no longer dine there in the evenings, or the five-course Sunday lunches to the families who are not permitted to gather there each week after Mass. Instead she is quarantined at home with her twins. She is permitted to go out only once a week, without her children, and only to the grocery store, pharmacy, or the doctor. Like all Italians, she must carry a document with her that shows her name, address, and other personal data, explaining where she is going and why. Italians can be stopped by the *carabinieri* at any time and ticketed or arrested if they do not comply. And otherwise, they are not allowed to go beyond their own driveway. Nicoletta's children are roller skating from the living room to the dining room in her house to entertain themselves. She is scared for the future, for the health of her children and for her elderly parents, and she is sad for her country, saying, "This is World War Three." Her laughter now is mixed with tears, and my arms ache to hug her close.

Crises seem to bring out people's true nature, and this crisis is no exception. My friends in Italy, in the midst of this catastrophe, continue to go about their lives, obeying orders, staying at home, watching terrible scenes of military trucks transporting coffins since there are no more spaces in the graveyards, learning of friends who are infected, or who have died. And yet, almost universally, they display only valor, strength, and fortitude.

The national news in the United States is now all about Italy and how the virus has caught fire. It is not only my husband and I who are concerned. All Americans are watching Italy from afar and we wonder at how the Italians will cope with the illness and the deaths. Daily, we see the viral videos of quarantined Italians singing from their balconies and rooftops, of a tenor performing "Nessun Dorma" as the sun sets over Florence ("*Vincerà!!*"—It will be won!!"), and a film of Italian military jets streaming the colors of the Italian flag in the afternoon sky over the ocean. Each one gives me shivers.

What I find most remarkable is that the Italian people are defined, more than anything else, by their connections to their families. And with this crisis, that is precisely what they are asked to do without. Italy, like Trattoria dell'Amicizia, is dark and shuttered. There are no Sunday lunches with the grandparents, brothers and sisters, new girlfriends, and new babies. No arguments over soccer and politics in the bars and cafes. No coffees after church. No church.

All of this goes against the very essence of what makes Italians, Italian. And yet they persevere. *Avanti, avanti*, they say. Forward. They do not whine or moan. They stay home. Grown-ups stop going to work. Children go to school virtually, on their computers. Grandparents and grandchildren connect only via phone. And the pope says Mass at St. Peter's Basilica, alone.

And now the drumbeat has become a violent symphony as the virus gets a grip in America. COVID-19 appears in Seattle, Washington, in New Rochelle, New York, and in California. The president, governors, and broadcasters everywhere speak of little else. The words "global pandemic" are finally uttered, and just like that, our whole world has changed. Schools are closed, events are canceled, and life as we know it is on hold.

The quarantine here in the United States is less restrictive and Americans are a little less willing to give up their liberties. But the fear is as real, as is the suffering, and the deaths are far higher than in Italy at its worst. It is our turn to go through the same surreal restructuring of our daily lives, using terms like "social distancing," "contact tracing," "PPE," and "antigen tests" as part of our lexicon. It is indeed a strange time. As of this moment, our flight to Italy has been canceled, pushed back and rescheduled five times. We are hopeful, expectant, even, that we will arrive back in Italy on July 9. We have our home and garden to look after, my husband's new vineyard to tend, and friends to see, if not to hold. But nothing is sure.

The hard work and austerity the Italians practiced so patiently has paid off. United as a country, they have turned the terrible upward curve of the pandemic back downward and seen the cases, the hospitalizations, and the death rate decline steeply. They are finally loosening restrictions and I picture them emerging from their homes, rubbing their eyes and blinking at the bright morning sun, stretching their arms upward and breathing in the fresh air. They deserve it. They have earned it. In the United States, the numbers are still on the rise and the future is uncertain. For months, our trip home to Italy has remained a shimmering, ephemeral vision on the horizon.

Finally, by midsummer, the case numbers in the United States and in Italy have dipped enough that a few flights begin to operate again. We take, literally, the second flight out of the United States to Italy, which is all but empty. Upon arrival, we quarantine completely for fourteen days, checking in with the health care authorities, recording our temperatures twice a day, and never leaving the yard. It has all been worth it. For months, cases have been plummeting, though they are on the rise in America, and we can enjoy many wonderful, restorative days here in our home, dining outdoors, living relatively normally. The only terrible part is encountering our friends and being unable to hug them.

There is one more bit of good news, one more glimmer of hope for the future. There was an election held in Roddino, and after decades of the same mayoral team running the commune's government, a new candidate challenged them and won. The new mayor is Gemma's son, Marco, an energetic, forward-thinking man with lots of ideas for our community. When a mayoral candidate runs, he or she brings with him a coalition of eight others, who also receive votes. The person with the second highest number of votes becomes vice mayor, and that person is none other than our amazing next-door neighbor Angela. She was as shocked by this as anyone, as she only joined the coalition to support Marco, and then suddenly found herself as his vice mayor. I could not be happier for her, for Roddino, and for the future. Not surprisingly, she performs her job with the humility, selflessness, and generosity with which she has lived her whole life. I feel so fortunate to call her and Biagio, and their whole family, friends.

As for Zef, he is busy helping my husband convert a cottage on our property to a small winery, in addition to the dozens of other projects he is working on in the area. And his smile spreads as much sunshine as ever. Up the hill in Roddino, Trattoria dell'Amicizia is open again, thank the Lord, and Nicoletta is back blessing us all with her flawless cuisine and unflagging friendship. Her twins are thriving and are now taller than she is. Piero and Innes, along with their daughter and granddaughter, are back cultivating their vegetable and flower gardens, setting aside plenty of *zucca* for next winter's minestrone.

August 2024: The pandemic has passed. Italy, Piemonte, Monforte, Roddino and the Langhe continue to thrive because of the remarkable people. They have endured world wars in their backyards, terrible dictators, devastating earthquakes, and plagues. The pandemic never stood a chance. I am cancer free and healthy. And Kim is looking forward to his fourth vintage of Barbera di Barbara.

Life, here in Italy, is sweet.

BOOK CLUB QUESTIONS TO SPARK DISCUSSION

1. In what ways does the process of dismantling a 300-year-old stone barn symbolize the author's desire for a fresh start and new beginnings? How does her project serve as a metaphor for personal growth and transformation?

2. Discuss the challenges and rewards of pursuing a dream, as illustrated by the author's journey of building a new life in Italy.

3. Reflect on the theme of home and belonging in the book. How does the author define home and what does it mean to them?

4. What is the overarching message or lesson that readers can take away from the author's memoir about building a dream and finding joy in unexpected places.

5. Have you ever felt a strong pull towards a place that made you reconsider your life choices, just like the author did when she found herself in Italy? How do you think you would adapt to the challenges and joys of living in a different country, away from your familiar home and routine?

6. Share a personal experience of embarking on a new adventure or project that brought about unexpected discoveries and pleasures, like the author's farmhouse restoration journey.

7. If you were to pick one recipe from the book to try, which one would it be, and why does it appeal to you?

8. Reflect on a time when you had to step out of your comfort zone, as the author did when she left her life in San Francisco to build a new home in Italy.

9. Share a story of an important relationship in your life that has evolved and grown stronger through shared experiences, similar to the author's bond with her husband.

10. Discuss a moment in the book that made you pause and reflect on your own dreams and aspirations. How did it inspire you?

11. If you could transport yourself to any moment in the author's story, which scene would you choose to experience firsthand, and why?

12. Reflect on a dream or passion project that you have always wanted to pursue. How does the author's story encourage you to take the first step towards making that dream a reality?

ACKNOWLEDGMENTS

Thank you to my editor, the accomplished Jane Rosenman, for her wit and wisdom throughout this project. Without her, there would be no book. Thank you, too, to the multi-talented Carolyn Muehlenbeck for her keen eye and unselfish guidance on the final edits, as well as her friendship from the very beginning of this adventure. To all the women at She Writes Press, Brooke Warner, Lauren Wise and especially my fellow authors, thank you for your unfailing support and advice. Grazie mille to Alice Rocchi, my brilliant Italian teacher, as well as to our dear friends here in Italy for the many kindnesses you have shown us. To my beautiful family, thank you for your love and patience over the years. Finally, thank you to Kim, for everything.

ABOUT THE AUTHOR

For years, Barbara Boyle enjoyed a colorful worldwide career as a Creative Director at Saatchi & Saatchi, Grey, Lowe and other advertising agencies, creating commercials and stories for Procter & Gamble, Johnson & Johnson, Mars Inc, and dozens of other marketers. Always a writer, this is the first time she has had the time required to author a book. Her flash fiction has appeared in *Sky Island Journal*, *Star 82 Review*, *Flash Fiction Magazine*, and other literary journals. Food and wine have also been a lifelong passion of hers. While living in Paris, she took the Regional French Cuisine course at Le Cordon Bleu and later completed the professional cooking course at The Institute of Culinary Education in New York. She now resides in a farmhouse in Piemonte, Italy, with her husband, Kim, surrounded by orchards, vineyards, and barking deer, and maintains a home in San Francisco.

barbaraboyleauthor.com

and : barbaraannboyle10

 : @barbaraboyle10

boyleb.substack.com

Author photo © Ivo Chiappello Photoemozione

Looking for your next great read?

We can help!

Visit www.shewritespress.com/next-read
or scan the QR code below for a list
of our recommended titles.

She Writes Press is an award-winning
independent publishing company founded to
serve women writers everywhere.